A Survival Guide For College and University Professors

JAY HETTIARACHCHY

A SURVIVAL GUIDE FOR COLLEGE AND UNIVERSITY PROFESSORS
Copyright © 2021 by Jay Hettiarachchy

All rights reserved. No part of this publication may be reproduced, distributed, or transmitted in any form or by any means, including photocopying, recording, or other electronic or mechanical methods, without the prior written permission of the publisher or author, except in the case of brief quotations embodied in critical reviews and certain other noncommercial uses permitted by copyright law.

Although every precaution has been taken to verify the accuracy of the information contained herein, the author and publisher assume no responsibility for any errors or omissions. No liability is assumed for damages that may result from the use of information contained within.

Library of Congress Control Number: 2021904000
ISBN-13: Paperback: 978-1-64749-383-7
Epub: 978-1-64749-384-4

Printed in the United States of America

GoTo Publish

GoToPublish LLC
1-888-337-1724
www. Gotopublish. Com
info@gotopublish. Com

CONTENTS

Preface vii
Introduction ix
   Chapter 1 Your First Teaching Job in a College or University 1
   Chapter 2 Learning on the job 7
   Chapter 3 Classroom Management 13
   Chapter 4 Faculty Evaluation 23
   Chapter 5 Faulty Tenure 33
   Chapter 6 Faculty Promotion 39
   Chapter 7 Faculty Service 47
   Chapter 8 From Teaching to College Administration 51
PART II 59
   Chapter 9 Teaching/Learning Resources 59
   Section 10 The Beginnings 61
   Section 11 Paradigm Shift 67
   Section 12 Teaming-up for Learning and Doing ... 77
   Section 13 Outcome-based Teaching and Learning 87
   Section 14 Critical Thinking 95
   Section 15 Epilogue 103
References 107
Appendix 1 109
Appendix II 117

This work is dedicated to my father and mother from whom I learned the value of education. I am also greatly indebted to all my teachers, students, family, friends and colleagues from whom I learned most of the practical lessons in life.

PREFACE

The author comes from a family of educators. His father was a professor of Sanskrit in Benares University in India during the 1920s. His brother was a professor and later a Vice Chancellor of University of Colombo, Sri Lanka. His wife has been a University Professor at University of Arkansas in Fayetteville, Arkansas for over 25 years at the time of writing this book.

The author retired as a professor emeritus in Computer Information Systems from Ferris State University in Michigan after having served over 25 years in several universities in the United States. He began his career in education at University of Ceylon (Sri Lanka) at Peradeniya, Sri Lanka, in the 1960s.

The primary reason and the incentive for writing this book is to share the life-time experiences of the author with readers who are interested in pursuing a career as educators in colleges and universities. The author had no guidelines, recipe books or instruction manuals for learning the best practices of the art of teaching in colleges and universities at the time he chose university teaching as his profession. This book contains a collection of valuable information kept by the author in the form of memoirs.

The second part of the book details practical guidelines and ideas that may help novices as well as other educators who are interested in facing challenges in teaching especially during and after the COVID-19 pandemic that has greatly impacted the traditional classroom teaching.

INTRODUCTION

Colleges and universities of today evolved from mediaeval European educational institutions, the origin of which can be traced back to the Christian cathedral schools or monastic schools which appear as early as the 6th century and were in service for hundreds of years before their formal establishment as universities.

Religious denominations established most early colleges in order to train ministers. Oxford and Cambridge universities in England, Harvard, College of William & Mary, Yale College, Princeton University, Brown University, Columbia University, University of Pennsylvania, and Rutgers University in the United States of America, are examples of early institutions of higher education that had religious beginnings.

The enrollment of students to the universities during the mediaeval age and the period following that era was restricted along the lines of their religious affiliations and denominations. These universities were funded by donors belonging to religious denominations and the curricula in these early universities were restricted to classical education and theology. The universities were isolated from the new potential clientele of business families enriched by industrialization.

During the following centuries, universities thrived in number, size and complexity all over the world as evident by their history that almost every university in the world is proud about. These early universities provided a model of higher education to the rest of the world. According to their history, most reputable universities of the world are a few centuries old.

During the period of their growth and development the focus of the university education, governance, funding, administration and complexity changed drastically. Except for a few universities catering for the needs of religious denominations most of the universities no longer had a focus on religion or had religious affiliations. They became secular institutions of higher education, funded by wealthy donors, land grants, state appropriations, and tuition-fees collected from the attending students.

Universities not only provided higher education in a variety of disciplines to young men and women but also became employers of qualified academicians, administrators, and all other personnel of service sectors needed to run a business operation. Most universities also housed thousands of resident students in dormitories, and the maintenance and upkeep of these buildings, provision of food, management and discipline of young men and women living in those dormitories became an essential part of the daily operation of these institutions of higher education. Colleges and universities practically became second homes for a large number of young men and women who spent a good number of years during their formative years of life in under-graduate and graduate schools in such educational institutions.

According to the National Center for Education Statistics December 2012, there were 4,599, 2-year and 4-year degree granting institutions in the United States of America (Source: http://nces.ed.gov/fastfacts/display.asp?id=84. The number of under-graduate and graduate students enrolled in public 2-year and 4-year colleges, private 2-year and 4-year colleges during the year 2013 were 17,487,475, including 2,097,511 graduate and 329,076 professional students.

As reported in the Bureau of Labor Statistics, there were 1.7 million post-secondary teachers in the U.S, of whom all were college or university faculty except for 159,700 graduate teaching assistants. Excluding graduate teaching assistants, the number of faculty in the US is therefore 1.54 million. (Source: http://www.quora.com/How-many-professors-are-there-in-the-United-States).

Although the remuneration of university professors was comparatively lower than that in high-ranking positions in corporations, academic positions in the universities attracted many young men and women who were interested in pursuing a career in higher education and were also research minded. The tenure system that provides job security to university professors and the independence that came with their profession that ranks them with the profession of judges made university profession very attractive to many who make career choices early in their life.

However, during the past 50 years significant changes in colleges and universities started to occur with the result that in the recent years a large proportion of the PhD holders in most disciplines have been unable to obtain tenure track jobs in colleges and universities. Although academic jobs have been viewed by many intellectuals as attractive and desirable, people with doctorates in sciences have started to trade the autonomy and intellectual freedom traditionally enjoyed by university professors for high-paying jobs in the industry. There is also the growing tendency in colleges and universities to replace well-paid professional positions with adjunct, temporary, and part-time positions and graduate student labor.

This book is not about providing the reader with an exhaustive account of the growth and development of universities in the United States. Nevertheless this brief introduction of the growth of colleges and universities is given as an introduction to the rest of the material covered in the book which is written in the hope that it would provide useful insights and valuable information to those young men and women who have a passion for a university academic career as a teacher, researcher and a service provider to the academy as well as to the wider community of education in which they live. Most workers, including university professors are learners on the job. The sooner one learns about doing any business, the chances are that they will be better equipped for survival in their job. The reason as to why the book is entitled as a survival guide.

CHAPTER 1
Your First Teaching Job in a College or University
Life can be an unending search

The very first thing a person who has had a life-long dream for finding an academic position in a college or university is to look for the availability of such positions that would fit her academic desire, preparation and experience. It could be sometimes extremely hard when one is trying to find the first job with no experience. Some universities have graduate programs allowing teaching assistantships to graduate students, and such teaching experience gained would certainly help. A person who has set up a goal to gain an academic position in a college or university should therefore plan a teaching assistantship or an internship that helps in finding a suitable position later in life rather than hurt by engaging in part time jobs that are totally unrelated to an academic career. In short, ones first job may not come easily and not necessarily be the ideal one but could pave the way to gain one or two years of essential and needed experience by working in related positions in temporary capacity for the intended position later on in life.

The best way to search for academic positions in colleges and universities is to regularly go through the Chronicle of Higher Education that publishes vacant positions in colleges and universities. These positions may not be in the same state where one is living. If one is willing to relocate, it would certainly broaden the available opportunities. Job search is a wider subject not discussed in detail in this chapter; suffice it to say that sending applications to several places where there are job opportunities would be a good idea. Most of the reputed colleges or universities advertising for available positions expect a formal application, a cover letter, a resume giving related work experience and at least three references. It is also a good idea to customize your cover letter and resume to match the requirements of the job as it appears in the job description. This is something that most applicants do not know or do not think about before sending an application for a job. Usually there are a large number of applicants for available positions; there will be a search committee that will carefully look at every application in detail. They will most probably prepare a decision table on which they match the job requirements and the strengths of applicants and rank them accordingly. The usual practice is to narrow down all applications to less than ten suitable candidates and have a telephone screening of candidates before selecting at least three candidates who are suitable for an in-person interview. Most colleges have career services that prepare students for resume writing and interviewing with prospective positions. Therefore, it is best that career-minded applicants should take advantage of these opportunities during their college days. It is best that you ask an experienced professional to go over your job application and the documents for comments and suggestions before you send an application in a hurry.

You could consider yourself very fortunate if you get to the point of being considered for an interview in person. Although it is not intended to write about good interviewing tips in this discussion, having had practical knowledge and experience in interviewing and gained good understanding about how to handle an interview with grace and confidence is definitely going to help. Remember, there will be others who are interviewing for the same position and you have no way of knowing how the others would perform or will have performed in a job interview in which you are also a candidate. So there is nothing to lose by doing your very best at the interview. At the very least you will have gained another experience in a live real-world interview and have gained a good understanding of what some colleges and universities are looking for in the teachers who they want to hire. One thing you need not forget is the time that an interview committee gives you for asking any questions you may have. It is best that you gather as much information about the college or university you are interviewing for a position prior to your interview and ask questions in such a way that you show the interviewers that you are going to be a contributor to the mission/vision of that institution rather than asking them about salary and other benefits that come with the job. Some interviewees do a great mistake in not asking any questions which clearly sends a signal that the person is not terribly passionate about the job she is applying for.

Please understand that your job interview is not similar to a just one-way street. As much as an institution has the right to interview you and ask all relevant questions about you and your qualifications to do the required job, you have the right to observe and ask at least some questions that are important to you about the type of job they expect you to do. Since you are going to make a decision to give a good part of your productive life to a place that you want to work for you got to make sure in your mind that it is the right place and right people you are going to work for. Remember, this is not the only place that wants you for your qualifications. There will be other places that could be better choices for you. The worst thing that could happen is that you get the job in a place that you hate to go to work every day. You do not want to be working at such places.

Having first hand information about a work place is certainly a good idea. This is where having friends or acquaintances who could give you both positive and negative information about a work-place is important. Usually, there is no way of knowing about the negative side of a work place in the interview process. You will hear all the positive things about a work place at the interview time, but unfortunately the reality could be very different after a person assumes work. This is because, the last person hired in a work places gets the most amount of work generating most number of credit hours in undergraduate colleges and universities. Information about the number of new faculty members hired in a college or university within the last few years would be helpful if one has any way of getting such information from those who are knowledgeable about the employment records of a workplace. Frequent advertisement for the same position year after year in Chronicle of Higher Education is another indication. Some small colleges having financial difficulties and facing enrollment decline do tend to engage in such hiring and firing practices during almost every academic year. Therefore, prospective candidates interviewing for academic positions in colleges/universities will have a careful and calculated decision to make whether to accept or reject a position offered to them in such a place.

Some college/university interviews spread over few days. They fly you over, pick you up at the airports, check you into hotels and put you on a presentation schedule, take you out for lunch and dinners where faculty members other than those in the search committee and sometimes their family members as well, have a chance of visiting with you and exchanging information with you in an informal and indirect way. These breakfast, lunch and dinner arrangements give them to ask informal questions, observe your manners, eating habits, and other personal information about you. Some colleges/universities arrange realtors to take you around the area and show you properties that you may want to buy in case you are hired. These are situations that you have to be guarding yourself against and be very diplomatic about in responding to the personal questions asked. The faculty members who are not in the search committee also have a chance to give their feedback and comments about you.

If you happened to be hired and if you decided to accept the job, it is also a good idea for new faculty members to live within close proximity to the college or university where they work. Walking distance to work will be the ideal situation if one has to teach 8:00 am classes, and/or night classes. Travel during winter semester could be hazardous. Some students who attend your classes may have to commute several miles. Such commuting students may find it very disappointing if a faculty member is absent due to bad weather.

The bottom line is, it is more difficult to keep a job than finding one unless one develops and practices skillful methods for managing difficult situations and know how to handle difficult people.

CHAPTER 2
Learning on the job

This chapter assumes that you were hired as a tenure track assistant professor position, which is the bottom rank of the academic faculty totem pole in most colleges and universities in the U.S. Some colleges have instructor, assistant lecturer, and lecturer, positions below assistant professor rank, but they are basically temporary positions that do not necessarily lead to an academic career and therefore not considered in this chapter. It is also assumed that the faculty member has been hired by a 4-year teaching college/university.

Most colleges and universities grant tenure to a faculty member hired for a tenure-track position in their sixth year depending on satisfactory performance on the job consistently in probationary capacity. Satisfactory job performance is discussed in the next chapter on faculty evaluation. Tenure and promotion are subjects discussed in two other chapters that follow. But first, this discussion is about what is expected of a brand new probationary faculty member in order to survive in a college/university teaching position.

Under normal circumstances, a faculty member in a 4-year teaching college or university is expected to teach 12 credit hours, which means teaching 4 courses of 3 credits. There could be 1 credit or 4 credit courses that are exceptions to this rule and are not considered for the purpose of this discussion. A rule of thumb is that no faculty member is expected to teach courses involving more than three new preparations; this means at least one of the courses taught could be a repeat course taken by a different set of students. You will probably see some senior faculty members teaching two repeat sections or four repeat sections of the same course that make up 12 credits as a full load. But you will have to wait for a long time to get to that place of comfort. In universities offering graduate programs, many senior faculty members teach a single course once in two years or none at all, and some faculty members get graduate assistants to do most of their teaching responsibilities. Our focus in this chapter is however on 4-year under-graduate teaching colleges or universities and therefore teaching in graduate colleges and universities is not included in this discussion.

The class size and the time of the class are other important issues. Early morning 8:00 am classes, lunch hour classes, late evening classes and weekend classes are not the favorites of most college/university professors. Some lucky professors will get their teaching for the week done within two or three days of the week that leaves them with two or three free days plus the weekends free. This is one reason as to why college/university teachers get bad reputation for not doing comparable work with other workers who do 40 hours of work within a week working from 8:00 – 4:00 pm with a lunch break of half hour. The justification for all the free time they have besides the time that they spend in classes and laboratories involved in teaching science classes, is that the preparation time for the classes by the instructors take many hours to gather new material involving reading of many books and researching on the subject matter. Nevertheless the reality of this is that not many undergraduate university professors except the novices spend all that time in preparing for their classes and they may not spend that much time in doing the teaching in the classroom either. With the availability and popularity of teaching software and courseware pre-packaged by leading book companies, most professors in undergraduate colleges and universities simply present packaged-teaching material available as Power Point Presentations prepared by book companies that sell text-books to college students. The process repeats almost every year with new revisions and new teaching material made available to college professors.

With online teaching and learning practices that are not only attractive to colleges and universities but also to students who are unable to be physically present in classrooms, some faculty members have started to teach a full load of courses online, sometime during weekends only. Although in theory, online courses should take more time and preparation including individual attention given to students on seven days at all times including providing online office hours, very few online teachers as well as students would admit or indeed strictly follow these practices.

All colleges and universities are not alike. They do not have a uniform set of rules, regulations and procedures. An examination of the handbooks containing those rules, regulations, and procedures of different colleges and universities in the same state as well as those belonging to the same university system, will confirm this observation. Some small colleges do have "invisible" rules and regulations that have more or less become a part of the culture of those institutions. A newcomer is well advised to first find out and then observe those invisible rules at work in order that s/he survives in such work environments.

But there are certain colleges and universities that mandate new faculty to go through an orientation program within the first semester of employment in addition to doing the teaching-load assigned to them. This is a good opportunity for a novice faculty member to meet with other new faculty members and to learn about the rules and regulations practiced in that institution. Many new faculty members however neglect to thoroughly study the handbook of the institution and understand all the rules, regulations and procedures that govern its employees. It is far better to know those rules ahead of time so that one can guard against mistakes that they may make unknowingly. This is because ignorance about those rules is not always considered as a valid excuse.

There are only 18 states at the time of writing this book that have strong education unions in the United States as shown in the following Google link: http://edexcellence.net/file/112268. It is unfortunate that many workers do not truly understand the pride and dignity of the work that they do. Workers unions are forums in which workers have a great opportunity to communicate with other union members on issues that are important to them collectively without being fearful to express their genuine concerns in their workers unions. Although there are negative aspects of workers' unions as well as abuse of union rights by workers, the benefits of unions are not altogether negligible. There are times when individual workers are singled out for mistreatment in many work places in which workers unions interfere for justice when injustice is apparent. It is a good experience for most workers who begin their careers to take a positive attitude about workers unions, at least to truly find out if unions are harmful to workers and the general public that organizations are supposed to serve. It is always a good idea for a novice worker to be affiliated with a union if there is one.

It is also most important that a new faculty member finds a mentor as early as possible in her/his new job. The mentor needs to be a trustworthy person who s/he could count on at all times. Such a person will be an invaluable resource providing guidelines regarding the expectations of a new faculty member, evaluation methods adopted, and other helpful ideas regarding the teaching philosophy adopted in that college or university. This is because it will be more difficult to do "damage control" after making mistakes by novices in a new work place. Therefore, a mentor, who cares for other peers at work and is passionate about her/his work, could be a useful ally for a beginner in any work place. Advice given by such a mentor would prevent most problems that new faculty members are bound to face especially during their probationary period at work.

CHAPTER 3
Classroom Management

Classroom management presents challenges to all teachers, especially those who are new to teaching. However, the degree of complexity of classroom management problems vary depending on the status of a college or university, class size, the status and rank of a teacher, her/his level of experience, the background and maturity level of students, and the "culture" of the educational institution. With the growing impact of technology in the classroom, additional classroom management issues will continue to challenge teachers. Therefore, it is extremely important that new college professors quickly learn the tricks of the trade in order that they do the least amount of mistakes on the job and be a survivor.

What is "Classroom Management?"

Classroom Management is a function of a teacher in a classroom with students. In an elementary school, grade school or a university, a teacher will be managing a class while performing the primary task of teaching; these tasks are not altogether mutually exclusive. A teacher's classroom management necessarily involves certain "house-keeping tasks" ranging from taking student attendance and maintaining discipline to planning and implementing meaningful curricula and lessons and evaluating and awarding a final grade for performance of every student who completed the course by attending the class.

Students learn the acceptable/appropriate classroom behavior during their grade-school years. Their physical presences in the classroom, as well as their interactions with other students and with their teacher, the purpose of their presence in a classroom, as well as the various written and unwritten rules, regulations, and policies and procedures that govern student and teacher interactions and relations, make classroom management necessary both on the part of the student and the teacher.

Most college professors, even though they may be the experts in the subject matter they are expected to teach, may not necessarily have teaching or managerial skills when they start to teach what they know for the first time in life. The majority of college and university professors learn the art of teaching and classroom management on the job as they continue to teach classes year after year. Even the experienced professors, who have lengthy service records as teachers, may be humble enough to admit that they developed their own classroom teaching styles and classroom management styles by following a trial and error method.

From a teacher's perspective, a classroom consists of a group of students who form an audience around her/him. The teacher has a considerable amount of power, authority, and control over her/his students. We occasionally hear about teachers who manage their classrooms like "dictators", and manipulate their students by various methods. We also hear about teachers having classroom management problems and/or teachers who have arguments and confrontations with students in classrooms, and about teachers who are removed from a classroom by the administrators due to their lack of classroom management skills. We also hear about "good teachers" and "bad teachers" from students. In larger colleges and universities where multiple sections of classes are offered by different teachers, most motivated students take extra efforts to sign up for classes taught by "good teachers" and avoid attending classes taught by "bad teachers".

Although the relationship between teacher and student has undergone considerable change over the years, there is still an understanding that a student is expected to perform the tasks required by a teacher who will award a grade for completing the tasks necessary in order to fulfill the requirements of a course. As reflected by the course syllabi that students receive on the very first day of a class at the very beginning of a course, a teacher and a student have a contractual relationship – the teacher is expected to teach, and the student is expected to learn. The teacher has the authority and obligation to evaluate and award a grade for a student's performance. A teacher can evaluate the performance of a student as "excellent," "satisfactory," "passing," or "failing." Looking at it from a student's standpoint, this relationship may possibly place the student in an adversarial relationship with a teacher.

Classroom Management in a Changing Classroom

Unlike in the past, today's educational institutions, whether they are private, corporate, non-profit, or government, are managed similar to any other business enterprise. Most college administrators are in severe competition with other educational institutions to increase the intake of eligible students due to cut backs on state and other funds on the one hand, and decreasing number of eligible students on the other. Consequently, students are considered as "customers", by most competitive colleges, like in any other business enterprise.

Faced with the challenge of finding creative ways of attracting and satisfying their "customers" in education, college administrators are attempting to enhance education with technology, since technology is supposed to enable cost reduction and increase productivity. Theoretically, utilization of technology is believed to decrease the cost of management of educational institutions and delivering cost effective education. Hence there is considerable efforts in educational institutions in recent years to "down-size", and "re-align" education administration and eliminate duplication of course offerings using technology.

A significant twist in education seen within the past decade is the large-scale expression of dissatisfaction with the traditional educational system by educators and education reformers. Whereas traditional teachers and the traditional methods of teaching are down played, innovative methods of teaching aided by technology are supported, enhanced and encouraged by most educational institutions. A comparison of the characteristics of traditional and the innovative teachers as portrayed by education reformers may be tabulated as follows:

Traditional teacher	Modern teacher
Controls students	Student centered
Manages (literally)	Does not manage
Strict/coercive	kind/flexible
Punishes/manipulates	No punishment
"Talking Head"	"Guide on the Side"

Causes stress	No stress
"Sage on the Stage"	Guides
Uses Chalk board	Uses Multimedia Teaching Tools
Syllabi driven	Outcome based
In-class teaching	partially online or 100%

Teachers who have lived a lifetime of traditional teaching and are caught up in the middle of these changes, openly express their desire to retire from their service and are relieved because they do not have to experience the uncertainties of the period of change and transition in education in the technological and information age. Many retiring and retired teachers are expressing their joy retiring after a lifetime of teaching, or retiring early with whatever retirement benefits they obtained at retirement. In a way, this portrays the gradual decline of one educational era and the emergence of another – the educational systems enhanced by technology, gradually replacing the traditional book-learning education system.

Supporting the educational institutions undergoing significant changes, are the "technology giants" entering into the educational software and hardware market with technological innovations that enhance education, by providing educators with "better tools to teach" and students with "better ways to learn." The recent tendency for high schools and colleges to make "universal access" with computers, distance education, and "virtual university" is an education innovation, attempting on one hand to provide more flexibility to education than under the traditional educational system, and reduce educational costs with technology on the other.

The phenomenal development of the Internet, and the World Wide Web, during the latter half of the 20th century, is probably one of the most significant contributing factors that have started to impact the educational arena in a most powerful way. It is against this background that the task of managing classroom becomes a most challenging job for today's teacher.

Obviously, today's teachers face students far different from those faced by their predecessors. These students have been exposed to a very powerful television media from their early childhood, and are also exposed to computers, smart phones and instant electronic communications methods from their childhood through grade-school days before they attend college. Consequently, the majority of college students entering colleges today have been exposed to the Internet and the World Wide Web. Therefore, the traditional methods of teaching are bound to be less effective in a classroom consisting of students belonging to the "information age." Most students who are computer and smart phone savvy will be having a hard time paying attention to college professor who uses traditional teaching methods. A newcomer who joins a college or a university as a professor need to be mindful of this change that is critical to classroom management for his/her survival in such a changing classroom environment.

A mixed class consisting of students belonging to the current generation, and adult students of the earlier generation, would place a teacher in a situation, having to find methods to satisfy different sets of students with different types of preparations and talents, gathered in the same classroom. Juggling between both these sets of students, in such a classroom and keeping both sets of students focused and satisfied, would certainly be a challenging, yet not an impossible task. Finding out what the needs of each student in a classroom on the very first day of a class is, therefore, of utmost importance for a teacher to establish a relationship based on caring and personal attention. In this regard, a sample of the responses given by students for the question "what makes me happy" on the very first day of a class is given in Appendix I. This is one of the many simple techniques the author used on a regular basis to establish a feedback system with his students in order that he could devote personal attention to student learning process. Obviously, it is not practicable for a teacher to establish such close relationships with a class consisting of hundreds of students. Some ingenious methods would be required by teachers of "Virtual Universities" to establish caring relationships with students who they most probably will never see in their lifetime.

Though proven to stand the test of time, the traditional methods of teaching may not deliver the desired results in the classroom of the information age. Today's distance-learning class, the electronic class, as well as the traditional class consisting of students who physically meet in a confined classroom, require different classroom management styles and strategies.

Depending on the composition of her/his audience, a teacher has to be able to adjust his/her role in a classroom as a teacher, a leader, a manager, and at times, an entertainer. For example, different types of students belonging to different disciplines, ranks, age groups, and preparation levels may be a challenging classroom for any teacher. Similarly, a classroom that meets at an odd hour of the day would require extra efforts, skills, and experience on the part of a teacher. A class of 600 students and a class of ten students would demand different management skills. Further, a group of passive students may require different skill set on the part of a teacher than a group of active students.

Some valuable insights for college/university professor's job:

In most traditional educational systems of the world, the teacher was considered as important or next in importance to a parent of a youngster. A teacher not only taught a "discipline", but was also a role model to a student. Besides the subject matter, a teacher also taught other values and morals to a student. The relationship between a teacher and a student was based on mutual respect, caring, and love. The teacher was there to teach and the student was there to learn. Since there was no "grading system" that "flunked" a student, the failure of a student, under such a system, also meant the failure of a teacher to "mold" a student in the same way as the failure of a parent in bringing up a child.

The "classroom management" issues, concerning students as well as teachers, discussed above are symptomatic of the current education system catered for the "mass-production" of students in colleges or universities. Under such a system, the relationship between a teacher and student may be based on criteria other than those under the traditional educational systems. Depending on the size of a class, a teacher may not be able to devote individual attention to every student. In general, the teacher-student relationship is simply a "contractual relationship" where the teacher is only a paid-employee of an educational institution and the student is a "customer" who the teacher has to satisfy.

However, in colleges where each student counts for their survival, satisfying students (customers), is of primary importance to an education administrators. In smaller colleges, therefore, a teacher would be more willing to provide individual attention to students, partly due to the smaller number of students they teach and partly because the retention of every student is important for the survival of the institution. In such a situation, a common teaching philosophy practiced by each faculty member, could reduce classroom management problems, and enhanced mutual respect between faculty members and students. Therefore, an uncoordinated teaching environment in which each teacher has her/his own different teaching philosophy, and style may only lead to dissatisfied customers (students) as well as dissatisfied and demoralized teachers (employees of college administrators).

Today's college/university professors need to understand that distance education, electronic classroom, and "the virtual university", have introduced complex and difficult classroom management challenges that are very different from those in a classroom where students and teachers all physically gathered in one location that we call a classroom. Only those professors who come up with innovative methods of managing such audiences without compromising the quality of education will be the survivors as teachers of the changing college/university of tomorrow.

CHAPTER 4
Faculty Evaluation

Faculty evaluation is critical for the survival of any new faculty member in a college or university that emphasizes teaching as well as research. This is because it can make or break the career dreams of a novice college/university professor who wants to build a career in the academy. This chapter on faculty evaluation is written in the hope that it would provide a clear understanding of the things to do and avoid by novice faculty members during their probationary period and thereafter as well.

The Process:

The evaluation process in most colleges and universities in America normally begins during the months of October/November. Most colleges and universities have a strict time schedule, processes and procedures as to how the faculty evaluations are conducted. Although the details of how evaluations are done may be different depending on the colleges and universities, the time schedule and the main activities involved in evaluating faculty members are generally similar. Most colleges and universities have faculty evaluation procedures clearly detailed in the faculty handbooks made available to every faculty member at the time when they are hired. Undoubtedly, it is supposedly the responsibility of university professor to study, learn, understand and be familiar with the material contained in those handbooks as they apply to their professional career.

Faculty evaluation methods followed in some small colleges:

The author gathered material for this writing by adopting the following methods: 1) informal discussions (I prefer to call these discussions rather than interviews) conducted within a period of five years with 15 faculty members. These discussions were done in a very informal manner and atmospheres in which the respondents concerned expressed their true feelings in a totally uninhibited manner. Some of the discussions were done in an unplanned manner, in grocery stores, during evening walks, at lunchtime etc., where the participants expressed their honest and genuine feelings from their hearts rather than formally with carefully chosen words. No notes were taken during these discussions as it was impractical. The discussions were intended to be non-threatening. 2) Faculty handbooks of several colleges and universities were referenced regarding various evaluation policies and procedures adopted by those institutions. Further, the evaluation procedures/practices adopted by four universities with which the author has had previous associations were closely examined. 3) The author also observed the evaluation practices adopted by one small college, within a period of five years. 4) Experience gained by the author from having been an active trade union member of three states for over 20 years.

These observations together with his experiences were helpful in making the analysis, comments, and observations made in this chapter. The chapter is written in the hope that it will have a positive impact on new college or university professors who have chosen teaching as a life-long professional career.

Faculty evaluation process in practice:

Following is a brief account in general of the evaluation process that takes place in the educational institutions. The details of the process will be different in different colleges and universities depending on the size of the college, culture and practices adopted over the years. The discussion is based on the commonalities of the practices adopted in three states, namely Minnesota, North Dakota, and Michigan.

1. The division head appoints evaluation committees. These committees consist of an evaluation committee chair and at least two other senior members of the department in which the faculty member to be evaluated serves. The chair of the evaluation committee summons a pre-evaluation meeting.

2. At the pre-evaluation meeting, the faculty members who are to be evaluated will agree upon class visits for each class that they teach. For instance, if there were 7 non-tenured faculty members who teach four different classes to be evaluated within that year, there will be 28 class visits that take 28 hours. Some classes, in this process are visited two or three times by different evaluators. In certain departments where there are only a few tenured senior faculty members, they

will be spending a significant amount of time going through the procedure of evaluating new faculty members every year.

3. Each instructor who is evaluated writes a self-evaluation that he/she submits to the evaluating committee.

4. The Division secretary visits each class taught by the faculty member who is evaluated and administers a questionnaire to the students, this process takes at least 20 minutes of class time. A secretary types each and every response and tabulates all the answers in summary form. (this takes class time plus several hours of secretarial time).

5. The evaluation committees meet "behind closed doors" to talk about each instructor that they "observed" in class. The head of the evaluation committee presents to the evaluation committee a completed evaluation forms at this meeting. The committee goes through student evaluations, tabulated student evaluations, student comments about the instructor under evaluation, and self-evaluation submitted by the instructor undergoing evaluation. The committee members review and discuss the above material concerning the faculty member under evaluation and make their recommendation for or against retention of that faculty (at least 7 X 3 or 21 hours are spent on this process).

6. Each faculty member evaluated is summoned to a post-evaluation meeting chaired by the

division head where the decision of the evaluation committee is informed in writing (approximately 2 and 1/2 hours).

7. The decision of the evaluation committee is then conveyed to an Academic Committee consisting of all division chairs and headed by the Academic Vice President of the institution.

   There could be variations of the formation of this academic body in different colleges/universities depending on the titles of various academic offices in those institutions.

8. The decision regarding the renewal/non-renewal, tenure or promotion, as the case may be, is conveyed in writing by the Vice President of Academic Affairs to the President of the college/university for a final recommendation to be sent by the President to the State Board of Higher Education.

Some reflections on the due process:

The independent evidence of several faculty members with whom the author had discussions regarding their personal experience and opinions on faculty evaluations revealed that the process, according to many faculty members who were willing to talk about heir evaluations, was very unfair, humiliating, threatening, degrading, and insulting. One faculty member decided not to go through the process for a second time since she thought it was too humiliating so she resigned her position as a faculty member. Unfortunately, not everybody is economically independent and confident enough to take such a decision in life. A retired professor who had served in one of the above universities for a long period of time and had served as a head of department, called the process a "bunch of crock." Another faculty member who went through the process for a second time mentioned that she was not offered a second year contract for reasons purely other than academic and teaching related. Another faculty member said that he was told to "keep his mouth shut" if he wanted a good recommendation in his next job search.

Many of these faculty members were fearful about their future, their family and children. They were too bitter about the situation and were happy to leave their job. Three persons who left their university careers expressed their bitter sentiments about the unfair treatment they received even after the passage of several years.

The evaluation process highly varies among different academic institutions depending on their "cultural setup." Even within the same institution, the process varies among different disciplines with regard to its implementation rules and regulations, procedures, and style. The process also differs with the personality traits and personality conflicts of the person/persons involved in performing such evaluations. For example, a coercive personality had used the process for "punishing" and/or "eliminating" a faculty member who s/he could not get along with. A jealous evaluator had used evaluation to remove a faculty member considered as a potential threat.

The discussions revealed that the officially recorded reason/s for terminating or "steering" a faculty member to resign could be very different from the "real reasons" which, on many occasions, were never truthfully revealed or never discussed by anybody other than those who were intimately involved in the process and directly affected by it.

Hardly any college professor would whole-heartedly agree that faculty evaluation is a pleasant experience. For many who have served in many academic environments and are not novices to the academic world and community and who have chosen to join lower ranks in the academic ladder for purely sharing their knowledge with the younger generation, evaluation of any sort could be repugnant, degrading, and humiliating. This is more so in the case of faculty who are independently wealthy (who do not have to work as college professors for a living), and who are proud of their educational qualifications, experience, teaching and other abilities and have chosen teaching as a profession primarily because of their passion for teaching and learning.

Some thoughts for novice professors:

New college/university professors who would want to survive as college professors have to face evaluation that may not necessarily be a pleasant experience whether they like it or not. They need to understand that their probationary period could be the hardest time of their career. During this period, they will have to carefully juggle while keeping the students happy on the one hand and keeping the evaluators happy on the other.

Unfortunately, probationary period of a new professor is the time when s/he has to keep every colleague happy including the head of the department. This is a time when a person has to compromise between her/his values, standards and at the same time walk a tight rope keeping a smiling face and being a nice person. This is a critical time when a new professor has to observe the "culture" of a new work place and learn what is acceptable and what is not in that culture before trying to implement new ideas and changes to existing systems. It is therefore prudent for new faculty to learn to live accepting the evaluation system of a given institution and live up to the expectations of the evaluators. Quick learners could learn these evaluation tricks every year as they go through the evaluation processes and experience.

Given below is an anecdote that one faculty member shared with me in my very first year of teaching in a university:

The professor who told me this story served in the mathematics department and he was a very strict teacher as most mathematics teachers are. One of his students was not in class to take the quiz given on that day and he gave zero for her for the quiz. The student walked to the office of the Dean of the Faculty of Sciences and told the dean that her boy friend has decided to break up with her and she had a hard time concentrating in class and therefore did not take the quiz. The Dean of the Faculty sent an open note to the mathematics professor who told me the story that stated, "you need to understand the traumatic experience of the student and allow her to repeat the quiz." During that year the Dean of the Faculty of Science sent a warning letter to the professor that he should try to improve his performance in teaching.

After this event, the professor who narrated his bitter experience made it a point to counsel those students who had traumatic experiences with their love affairs, and his performance evaluations improved thereafter, he added.

The anecdote clearly indicates the difficulties faced by many faculty members in small colleges and universities in trying to maintain education standards while the administration is trying to increase and retain the number of students in those institutions. Getting a feel for the culture in which a college or university operates as well as the "politics" of a given place tends to be critical for new professors who want to survive amidst conflicting expectations of college administrators, peers, students and personal convictions.

CHAPTER 5
Faulty Tenure

College/University academic careers are attractive to hard working educators who also have a passion for research and discovery as well as imparting of the knowledge they have gained over the years to others who are interested in learning and propagating knowledge. Although tenure is an attraction for new professors to select college and university careers as their lifetime job, it can also be a nightmare of six years depending on how tenure is given in certain colleges and universities.

Notwithstanding its negative aspects the tenure system has been known as the holy grail of the teaching profession. According to American Association of University Professors (AAUP), tenure is an arrangement whereby faculty members, after successful completion of a period of probationary service, can be dismissed only for adequate cause or other possible circumstances and only after a hearing before a faculty committee (http://www.aaup.org/issues/tenure). This is a privilege that does not come with most other jobs in other industries and businesses in which job security can be stressful for career-minded people who seek life-time jobs in a peaceful work environment.

Since its inception in 1915 American Association of University Professors has assumed responsibility for developing standards and practices, sometimes in cooperation with other organizations, to give concrete meaning to tenure. Interested readers may refer to the following AAUP tenure policy statements for a complete understanding of the origin and development of the tenure system of universities in North America:

1. 1940 Statement of Principles on Academic Freedom and Tenure (http://www.aaup.org/report/1940-statement-principles-academic-freedom-and-tenure)

2. the 1958 Statement on Procedural Standards in Faculty Dismissal Proceedings (http://www.aaup.org/report/statement-procedural-standards-faculty-dismissal-proceedings) and

3. Recommended Institutional Regulations on Academic Freedom and Tenure (http://www.aaup.org/report/recommended-institutional-regulations-academic-freedom-and-tenure)

In most unionized states academic freedom plus job security are packaged together into a union contract. Each college or university in the United States has a handbook that contains rules and regulations governing the tenure system among other administrative rules and regulations of that institution. Nevertheless, these handbooks are constantly changing with time with the result that in some colleges and universities such guidelines not only lack uniformity across the board, they are subject to changes and different interpretations of those who have the final say and power to implement them in those institutions.

Some realities about the tenure system

College and university tenure system has been a controversial issue that comes up in educational circles especially during times when there is a downturn in the economy. There are several reasons for such a controversy among educators and others who are interested as evident in educational circles, trade unions, newspaper publications, books written on tenure by educators and other publications appearing in journals such as the Chronicle of Higher Education.

A review of these sources reveals that the tenure system is not equally administered across the board in all the colleges and universities in the United States. For example, the standards and rigor applied to determine if a probationary faculty member is eligible to be tenured varies significantly among under-graduate and graduate higher educational institutions. Most of them require 6-7 years of probationary faculty service, and within this time probationary faculty members are annually evaluated by committees consisting of, at least three, senior faculty members. During this probationary period a new faculty member could find his/her career to be very insecure because s/he could be fired due to any reason ranging from poor work performance or economic hardships of the institution. Obtaining tenure could become harder as part-time, temporary, adjunct categories of teachers keep growing and the number of qualified recently graduated educators eligible for college teaching keeps increasing, and the available number of tenured positions in educational institutions keep decreasing.

Consequently, gaining tenure in colleges and universities has become increasingly difficult at least in a growing number of disciplines. Reorganization, re-alignment, downsizing, and structural changes in educational institutions are other reasons for reducing the number of tenured and senior faculty of many colleges and universities. Therefore, the popularly held belief that university professors have a permanently lifetime job is far from reality. Nevertheless, in reputed land grant or Ivy league universities there is a tendency to hire the most productive educators and research-minded faculty members and grant them the tenure status that they earn in those universities. Obtaining tenure having gone through the tenure process could be very hard for a new faculty member in any college or university; it could be harder in most reputed and leading universities in which carrying out research, publication of research findings in refereed journals, and raising funds for research are rigorous and highly competitive. In most mid-sized small colleges also teaching, service as well as research are used as the main criteria for evaluating a new probationary faculty member over a period of six years for granting tenure. Smaller teaching universities focus mostly on a faculty member's ability to teach effectively rather than their ability to do research and publications. Many of these colleges and universities do not even have the necessary equipment or laboratories suitable for doing scientific research. Under normal circumstances, new faculty members are given service courses to teach within their initial service years. These service courses are credit generators for a discipline/department and therefore teachers who are capable of keeping large classes having as many as 30 or more students happy are considered good teachers. Nevertheless, this could be a very difficult task considering the different preparation levels of students in any given class and the enthusiasm of students to learn the material covered in a course. Considering the above challenges, one important point any novice teacher should keep in mind is that the negative comments given by students in a class survey are taken more seriously by the tenure evaluation committees.

Probationary faculty members who are retained for a second and third year are given student advisement tasks in addition to a teaching load of 12 credit hours. If a faculty member takes advisement seriously and visits with each student assigned for his/her advisement, it takes a considerable amount of time and effort to keep track of the progress of advisees depending upon the number of advisees assigned. Comments made by advisees regarding his/her advisor also provide important information regarding tenure decision of a probationary faculty member in some colleges and universities.

The third important criterion in making a determination on the tenure of a probationer is the service provided by that faculty member to the department, college or the university as a whole, and the community in which the college or the university is situated. Such services could be voluntary or mandatory depending on the college or university requirements and traditions of any given college or university. For example, class projects involving service to the community is a good way of getting community members and businesses excited and involved about newer ways of doing things, especially in the agriculture sector.

The six probationary years are also a time when a new faculty member is judged by the other faculty members in a department as well as the faculty members at large in a college or university. In some colleges and universities, the opinions of the department members about the tenure decision are confidentially requested before a tenure decision is taken by the entire department. This rigorous process continued for 6 years shows that gaining tenure by a novice is not an easy task in most colleges and universities and it is an extremely difficult task in most of the reputed and Ivy league universities.

Contrary to the popular belief, tenure is not the greatest achievement of a college/university professor. Tenure simply gives them the security and confidence and ample time and resources that most independent thinkers need to do a good job of what they do as teachers and researchers in the academy without being fearful of losing their job and/or distracted by constantly having to worry about getting fired in their current job and having to worry about finding a suitable job the next year the year after. Tenure, as shown in the following chapter on promotion, is just a stepping stone to reach higher aspirations, satisfaction, recognition, and reputation to hard working academicians nationally and internationally among the community of learners.

Tenure gained in one academic institution is not generally transferrable and accepted by another academic institution unless it is negotiated and accepted at the time of a job offer with tenure and acceptance.

CHAPTER 6
Faculty Promotion

Unlike tenure that provides a firmer assurance regarding job security of an academic professional in a college or university, promotion is a recognition of academic or research achievements of an academic who has chosen her/his life-long profession as a college or university professor. Although the title "professor" is used in general to signify any college/university teacher, the term professor is used more specifically to identify the highest academic rank and status of a college/university teacher. Instructor, Assistant Lecturer, Lecturer, Assistant Professor, Associate Professor, Full Professor (Professor), University Professor, Distinguish professor are such ranks and titles given to college/university teachers depending on the status, renown and reputation of a college or university, as those who hold these positions rise up in the career ladder and are promoted to higher ranks of recognition in service.

Promotion is however not automatic. A university teacher has to earn his/her promotion by following a rigorous process as stipulated differently by different academic institutions. In certain situations, some hardworking individuals who have dedicated their entire life to academic careers and pursuits face difficult and unprecedented challenges in getting promoted to higher ranks in their profession even after having followed the policies and procedures very meticulously depending on the college or university in which they serve and seek promotion in their professional career. This is because the award and denial of promotion in many colleges and universities tend to happen in a very unpredictable way depending on the time, personality of the applicant as well as those of the administrators who have the power to grant or deny promotion to an applicant. Factors such as inter-personal jealousies, prejudices, adversarial personal relationships, likes and dislikes gender and ethnicity etc. that affect most human relationships too do contribute significantly in promotion decisions in very subtle or covert ways in seats of higher education as well. Such instances are openly discussed in union member forums of academic institutions and are privy to union members only. There are tricks and traps in every workplace including academic institutions regarding many critical institutional decisions and this chapter will shed some useful light on areas of difficulties that a novices or even experienced academic professionals are likely to face in their profession when seeking promotion.

Tenure, promotion, and salary associated with academic positions in colleges and universities are mostly determined by the ultimate governing body of those institutions.

In particular, promotion is tied up with a salary increase for those who get promoted in their positions. Detailed information about individual salaries of professors is generally not easily accessible to other workers except in the unionized work places including educational institutions. Moreover, the professional status of an academic teacher remains with the institution while s/he continues to serve that institution. The professional titles such as "full-professor" belong to the institution as long as the person who holds that title continues to serve in that institution. Only the educational qualification, publications, research findings and the patents owned by an individual remains with that person after s/he severs employment. In the case of private companies, however, the patents belong to the company and the person who discover that resulted in the patent does not have a right to own the patent. Only in the case of retired persons who satisfy all requirements for retirement as stipulated by the institutional regulations and gained emeriti status as a professor, s/he could use the professional status for whatever reason. Therefore, there is a great desire on the part of most workers to be strongly associated with an institution and work titles they hold in those institutions since the type of work that they do provide them with self-esteem, prestige and social status as well. As a result, recognition of their professional status with titles such as professor at work is most important for most individuals. The general tendency is therefore for most college/university teachers to aim to rise up to the highest rank in their profession.

In reality and practice however, tenure and promotion are control mechanisms that academic institution administrators use to increase productivity of their workers (teachers and researchers in this case). This control mechanism works in a similar but slightly hidden fashion in academic institutions than in private companies in which hiring and firing as well as job changes takes place in quick succession. While the firing of inefficient employees with immediate effect gives the private employer to hire more efficient employees quickly, the promotion of productive teachers and denial of promotion to others considered less productive give similar power and control to academic administrators over the academic professionals in a covert fashion.

Promotion Process:

All colleges and universities have timelines, policies, procedures as well as unwritten traditions to be followed by academic professionals in order that they gain promotion in their rank of service. While these policies and procedures are contained in the handbooks of every college and university, the unwritten traditions can be as important in the decision-making process depending on the strength and reputation of a given academic institution. The unwritten policies and procedures have a way of coming to surface depending on the applicants and the administrators involved in the process. One way of finding out of the existence of such a situation is by listening to those who had been denied promotion in their job and are willing to talk about it candidly and openly. But most academic professionals are unwilling to talk about the unfair way their case was dealt with by their institutions knowing that they have no chance to reverse promotions decision once taken. Some of them would rather quietly leave the institution while they can in a respectable way.

The promotion process is initiated by an applicant who is desirous to be promoted. Such an attempt is initiated by the interested party with the head of the department. This is because some of the information such as the allowable quota of promotions in a given college of study and the funds available are known to the administrators who have also access to the pool of eligible candidates and their seniority within a given year. The administrators therefore have better control over the process and are able to guide the process than the qualified applicants who may very strongly feel that they deserve to be promoted. Moreover, the head of a department in an academic institution tends to have a great deal of power at every stage of the promotion process. They certainly do have the capacity to steer the direction of the process positively or negatively in the promotion process. Therefore, it will be a prudent idea for a person seeking promotion to consult the chairman or head of a department before submitting an application. This is because the success or failure of getting promoted by a professor in a department greatly depends on her/his favorable or unfavorable personal/professional relationship with the head or chairman. Although it is possible for a faculty member to apply for promotion against the wishes of his/her administrative head, it will be a good idea to work with one's superiors than without such support. But, in cases where the interpersonal relationship of the head and the subordinate/s have become very adversarial beyond repair, it would be far better for a person to wait until his/her supervisor leaves the institution. Such occurrences are not uncommon or unusual in many academic seats of higher education. The reader may be in a position to relate to his/her personal experiences depending on the number of educational institutions and years of service put in for higher education by him or her.

Assuming that the applicant for promotion has no adversarial relationships with her/his head of department and gained the approval to go ahead with the application process, s/he has a substantial amount of task ahead to gather all necessary required supporting paperwork. Although the college/university handbooks provide general information about the type of support material needed, the guidance of a mentor who is very familiar with the details of the paper collection and the process of evaluation and who is genuinely interested in helping her/his co-workers to succeed professionally, could be of great help for most novice applicants for promotion. Therefore, it is very important that one has trustworthy co-workers who would be genuinely interested in helping others to succeed at work together. Under normal circumstances, this is not the case in academic institutions in which competition for limited resources is the prevailing trend. Nevertheless, if you are a good observer of your co-workers and their attitude towards other workers, you will be able to find helpful people in any given work place including academic institutions. In general there is a real need for co-workers in any work place that include seats of higher learning where highly educated and competitive people work, to support one another and promote an abundance mentality not only for promotion purposes for individual workers, but for the overall success of an institution as a whole.

In most colleges, a promotion portfolio of an applicant who seeks promotion should address the following three components: teaching, research and service. In detail these could be expanded to include:

- teaching philosophy and practices
- student evaluations of each successive year of service
- peer evaluations
- documents supporting research work done by the applicant including, publications, conferences attended and presentations made
- service to the institution
- service to the community

It is a good idea for a novice applicant to examine previous portfolios submitted by others who were promoted by the same institution to find out what the evaluators expect and how the criteria need to be compiled, organized, communicated, and presented effectively. Obviously, putting a promotion portfolio together in a hurry is not as helpful as writing the first draft and showing it to a helpful mentor or a trust-worthy colleague for comments, suggestions and modifications. This means, that one has to spend a great amount of time to gather material, compile them, and present them in an organized and effective way. In short, one's ability to solicit advise from trustworthy and experienced senior co-workers, organize write and present the material effectively, can almost guarantee success to a great extent.

For certain types of promotion beyond Full Professor in most universities, letters written by outside professional experts in an applicant's field are scrutinized by committees mainly consisting of administrative heads who are not familiar with research. These administrators have the final say in the decision making process. Such decisions are made by administrators behind closed doors giving no room for recourse by the affected party. Such things do happen in seats of higher education sometimes justly and sometimes unjustly. This is when educators who have dedicated their entire life for research, teaching and service keep wondering as to what harm they have done to the progress of knowledge in order that they deserve the way in which they are treated by denial of the recognition they have already achieved.

CHAPTER 7
Faculty Service

There are three types of workers: those who sponge on the work place like parasites, those who are married to the work-place and have no life and never have a life for themselves, and those who grow together with the work place being an asset to any work place for which they render their service.

A career minded person who is an efficient worker will be a contributor and asset to any work place. Such a person is a survivor who would be missed if he/she happens to leave work for personal reasons or retirement.

In a college or university, faculty service begins at the department level; the very bottom place a new faculty member is able to render his/her services. Some of these services are available to faculty members who hold tenure track positions only. Also, faculty members on tenure-track need to put in at least two years of service in a department to qualify for rendering such services. Some services are mandatory while others can be voluntary. Student advisement could be a mandatory service that each faculty member should be providing to students majoring in a department such as Mathematics, Physics etc. Depending on the college or university tradition there may be several service opportunities for new faculty members who volunteer to serve on departmental committees. Curriculum revision committee is one such example.

The normal human tendency is to do only those things in life that are absolutely necessary in life and try to avoid doing other work as far as possible. This applies to work life as well in case of most workers. The general attitude of workers is to avoid doing extra work that do not provide any career benefits or personal benefits, and consider such work as thankless jobs. However, when a person is building a life-long career, it is important to devote as much time getting involved in as many tasks as possible because this is one place in which a new faculty member starting his career in a college or university has immense opportunities to learn his/her business, meet with other faculty members, share ideas, accept leadership positions, be visible at the work-place and make a significant contribution at work. Such contributions accumulate similar to investments in a savings account that multiplies with compounded interest with time.

There are advantages to working in smaller colleges or universities in which 100 – 500 faculty members serve. This is because the larger the number of the work-force at a work place and greater the competition for the fewer opportunities available, it would be more difficult for a new comer to be visible unless he/she is extremely aggressive. But that is no reason for a new faculty member to be complacent even in larger colleges or universities waiting for things to happen someday.

The opportunities for serving a college or university multiplies when a faculty member puts in several years of service after gaining tenure. There will be opportunities to serve in department committees such as tenure and promotion committees, search committees to hire new faculty members to the department, and occasionally to hire chairmen or heads of departments. Then there will be opportunities for faculty members to represent their departments in a faculty/college senate or university-wide committees depending on the structure of the institution. Those faculty members who serve in these service positions get noticed and recognized by the college/university faculty and administrators due to the contribution they make while at the same time they gain experience in learning to do their work better and learn to hold and gain experience in leadership roles.

Although faculty service reviews are not available in the public domain, it will be good for an interested faculty member to go through the faculty service review of a close friend or a mentor who would be willing to share her/his faculty service review. Also, the type of letters of recommendation written by colleagues at the same work place and outside professionals who are familiar with ones work will give you a clear idea as to the type of things that a faculty member should be investing his or her time in performing faculty service in order that s/he improves her career prospects continuously.

Serving in departmental committees, faculty associations, and faculty senates could lead to serving in more responsible positions in the capacity of chairman of committees, secretary of faculty association and faculty senate as well as in the role of the president of faculty association and faculty senate of a college or a university. A faculty member who has gained experience in serving in such capacities makes her/him invaluable asset to an educational institution. Therefore, it is very important that a faculty member makes a conscious effort not to neglect institutional service as he/she builds her/his career. This is one unmistakable way of building a marketable resume as well enabling such a person to be recruited for a better position in a more lucrative environment for a higher remuneration. This is the reason for many senior faculty members to be in the lookout for more attractive positions, especially as academic administrators as shown in the next chapter.

CHAPTER 8
From Teaching to College Administration

This chapter is for those educators who are more interested in administrative tasks than teaching or are interested in trying out administrative positions in education to see if they like administrative tasks better than classroom teaching.

The most important three renewable resources college/university professors have in academic life are: 1) the young students who they meet and interact with as education recipients in their classrooms every successive year, 2) the renewing knowledge enhanced by research that they are transmitting to the young generation in their classes, and the peaceful time available for the pursuit of research and education, and 3) educational resources that they have at their disposal in a peaceful educational atmosphere. This, in a way, is a luxury that most educators enjoy as they work and share the fruits of their work in academic conferences nationally as well as internationally.

Nonetheless, some college professors choose to become college administrators as they put in long years of service as teachers whereas other professors are contented with teaching, research, service and the contribution they make to mankind as educators as long as they reach their retirement. They consider that full-professor position in a college or university is the highest position an educator could earn. Nevertheless, there are educators who would be interested in other things such as a higher pay for their service, liking for power, prestige, and control that comes with a job, and a liking for what they do as administrators without having to spend their time in learning, doing research, and disseminating knowledge. They could also be unhappy with teaching students year after year. The readers who have been in both teaching and administrative positions over long periods of time may have their own ideas about as to why they chose one type of job over the other in colleges they served. The ideas discussed below are for those young graduates who look for joining academic institutions with an open mind and a desire to join administrative positions with higher pay and power in the positions they hold in an institution.

The bottom rank of professor/administrator is the chairman or head of a department. The next higher levels of the hierarchy are: Dean of a faculty/college, Vice-President, (Vice-Chancellor), President (Chancellor) Provost etc. Depending on the size of a college/university system, there could be hundreds of administrative position in a single educational institution/system. A Google search on the organization chart of any given college or university will reveal the number of administrative positions as well as the titles and responsibilities of those who hold such positions.

Unlike teaching positions, administrative positions have stricter job descriptions depending on the size and status of a college/university. The positions also are well structured that require supervisory control and reporting tasks, in certain ways similar to those in private sector in which hiring and firing do take place in quick succession. An inefficient and unproductive person in such a set up would find her/his job very stressful unlike in a teaching or research job where performance on the job is not as critical for day-to-day survival in the job. Nevertheless, the benefits of administrative jobs in educational institutions of those who are capable of handling the requirements of those positions can be attractive to certain individuals whose personality is in alignment with stressful job situations. For this reason, some educators choose to be education administrators as they mature in service and are experienced teachers and at the same time tired of teaching and being underpaid for the type of service they provide. There is also the advantage of tenured faculty members to join administrative positions and keeping the tenure status in case they want to step down to their teaching position later depending on unforeseen changes that may take place in the college/university policy and structure. There are reported instances of those administrators who are stepping down to teaching positions keeping the same salary or accepting a reduced salary higher than the faculty salary they received while they held a faculty teaching position.

The opportunities for those teachers who are interested in administrative tasks while they are faculty members arise when a search for head of department position occurs. The search may end up in selecting an internal candidate over an outside candidate. Many administrators begin their administrative career by becoming a temporary or interim head of department in the same department in which s/he served as a member. Once a member of the same department selected as the head in the same department and after having served as an interim head for a few years, s/he will be eligible to apply for other available head of department positions in bigger and better colleges/universities with the experience gained as an education administrator.

Unlike most 9-month-teaching jobs in colleges, administrative jobs are 12-month positions that require 8:00 am to 5:00 pm work with a one-hour lunch break. They have the advantage of participating in training programs that prepare them for doing their job as administrators more effectively and efficiently. Most people who get into administrative positions tend to modify their behavior and personality and character as a result of the administrative training they go through. Suffice it to say that they develop a thick skin to handle difficult problems successfully. With the training they receive every successive year and with the experience they gain by interacting with other experienced administrators on the job by facing challenges that require decision-making and implementing as well as achieving the targeted results, they become better administrators with greater confidence over time. This is when they are ready to move into higher administrative positions that involve more power and responsibility not necessarily at the same place where they work.

After serving as a head of department, most enthusiastic people who are not satisfied with being a head of department want to move into higher levels of administration. The next level is a Dean's position of a college. Again, there are opportunities for heads of department of colleges to apply for vacancies of Dean's positions. Depending on the level of active participation of a head of department in a college s/he may have a better chance of getting recruited as a Dean of a college than a candidate competing from outside. A person's leadership style, personality, and charisma play a very significant role in being able to rise up in administrative positions and at the same time being able to effectively perform her/his administrative tasks. It goes without saying that good administration like good politics is an art and those who master it with grace become successful administrators. They also know that part of being a good administrator is not to serve in one place over a long period of time. Most successful administrators move from one place to another without stagnating too long at the same place and on the same position. The type of job they do, give them ample opportunities to interact with other colleges and universities that are more attractive to serve when an opportunities arise.

Also, Deans of colleges or universities accept similar positions or higher positions in other colleges or universities when the position they hold become insecure or they are given time to leave their current job due to personality issues, job performance related issues, or economic issues. The chances are that those who held teaching positions before very rarely step down to teaching positions. This is because they feel less well prepared, depending on the gap in service, to resume their previous teaching/research work if they get back to their former teaching position again. But there are some instances when heads of department get back to their former teaching positions do keep the same salary and wield greater power and influence in their former departments if and when they step back to their former teaching positions. Such people usually have the backing and support from other administrators who they once worked as their colleagues.

The next step in the administrative ladder is Vice Chancellor/Vice President of a college or University. The organization charts of colleges/universities give a clear idea as to how the administrative structures are organized with the power and reporting structures and the responsibilities associated with those who hold those positions. As one rises up to the higher levels of administration, the duties become more or less supervisory with more responsibility, power and influence. Some Colleges and Universities have several Vice Chancellors/Vice Presidents in each area of study labeled as Faculties or Colleges or Campuses. Each of those Vice Chancellors/Vice Presidents reports to the Chancellor/President/Provost/CEO of the institution.

The title of the highest administrative position in academic institutions is somewhat confusing. In most stand-alone universities and colleges in the United States, the chief executive officer is called the President and the second in command is called the Provost. In some multi-campus state university systems, like in the university system of North Dakota the Chancellor has authority over all universities in the system, and therefore ranks higher than the Presidents of individual universities within the system. In other state university systems, the President has authority over multiple campuses, each of which is headed by a Chancellor who come under the authority of a President. Catholic educational institutions name their highest administrators as Rectors.

Irrespective of the titles they hold, the top most position of College/University administration is the highest rank a person could hold similar to a CEO position in private industry. Not only does this position carry a substantial salary but it also gives them power and responsibility and dignity. This could be a job more political than educational that demands much from its bearer. Responsibilities of this position typically include fund-raising, establishing and maintaining connections with local government and balancing a number of constituencies like students, parents and alumni. It also involves providing leadership, delegating and supervising the implementation of all functions of the mission and vision of the institution and decision-making power regarding the long-range planning of the institution. The National Association of Independent Colleges and Universities maintains that the stresses involved with the position and the unique skill set required of college presidents forces schools to make lucrative offers to lure and hold onto talented executives. "Searches for these positions at a significant number of independent institutions are highly competitive, and colleges must offer compensation packages that attract qualified leaders," the NAICU said in a statement. (source: http://www.usnews.com/education/best-colleges/articles/2011/02/15/how-much-is-your-college-president-costing-you-college-president-cost-per-student).

Most academic professionals whether they are in the business of teaching students or are in administration, begin their service in education as teachers. There may be rare exceptions when academic institutions hire administrators from outside the academic arena and classroom teachers from private enterprises. But the general tendency is for both the academically minded teachers and education administrators to begin and pursue a lifelong career in educational institutions. Therefore a novice may need to make a choice early in life as to whether s/he wants to be an educator per se or an education administrator.

PART II
Teaching/Learning Resources

SECTION ONE
The Beginnings

The primary reason and the incentive of the author for writing this book is to share his life-long experiences with readers who are interested in pursuing a career as an educator in colleges and universities. The author had to learn his lessons the hard way. There were no guidelines, recipe books or instruction manuals at the time he began his teaching career to learn the best practices of the art of teaching in collages and successfully facing the challenges of transferring his knowledge to novices in the academic world.

How do we learn the best practices? One way is to imitate our teachers. In our life-time as students, we come across many different teachers, those who we like and those who we do not very much like. It is most natural that we tend to imitate the teachers that we like most. Another way of learning is trial and error method, in other words, to learn the best practices on the job by making mistakes on the way. Depending on one's personality and the level of confidence, one may choose either of these methods or any other methods or combination of teaching methods with which s/he is comfortable imparting knowledge to others.

Different disciplines call for different types of teaching methods. For instance, a mathematics teacher may have to have a different set of skills for imparting his/her knowledge to others than a language or history teacher or a professor of law. The author developed his own methods of teaching that he practiced over several years fine-tuning those practices by trial and error. He had the advantage of learning in several widely different disciplines, teaching history, sociology, natural languages, and computer science/computer information systems over a period of 42 years. Bridging those disciplines in imparting knowledge was a challenge as well as an advantage.

The author's very first class in Colombo Sri Lanka (university of Ceylon at the time) in 1967had about 1200 students. For a person beginning his career as a brand new teacher, a class of 1200 students gathered in a stadium previously constructed as a grand stand for viewing horse racing by the British rulers in Ceylon (Sri Lanka of today), was a formidable challenge. He had no choice of selecting a smaller class in his very first job than to lecture from a podium to an audience gathered several hundreds of feet away from him in the grand stand to listen to his lecture.

There was no visual aid to teach in this stadium. Using a chalk board would not have been feasible either. But the general thinking of the time was that a large class room, a teacher, and a chalk board were sufficient to teach liberal arts subjects, unlike science subjects.

However, my thinking about imparting knowledge was rather different. This was because getting students to think was more difficult than trying to impose on them my own way of thinking by a formal lecture. I therefore, had real hard time with the way I had to reach thousands of students gathered in a stadium using a public address system. Consequently, I found lecturing in a stadium as the most distressful thing that happened to me. It was not efficient, neither was it effective. I wanted to be closer to the students when I was trying to teach something to them as a teacher by listening to them and interacting with them. As for me, the grand stand was a hindrance for education. I had no idea how it felt like for my students sitting in a grand stand bleachers on a windy, rainy or a cold day listening to a lecture.

The newly constructed cubicles with metal roofs and open on one side exposing students to the hot sun, blowing winds and rain into those cubicles hardly satisfied the requirements of classrooms. They were merely temporary sheds hurriedly built for students who attended tutorial classes. They did not provide a suitable learning environment especially during hot, cold, rainy or windy days. However, in the tutorial classes I got to see the faces of the students closer and a chance to interact with them in person. If faces were mirroring the inner feelings of people, certainly there was more unhappiness in those faces of those students attending tutorial classes in cubicles than any happiness. Those students sitting and sweating in 90 degree hot temperature in tutorial classes were not at all in a mood to discuss tutorial topics; rather they were waiting to get out of the class as soon as they were allowed to.

As for me, this provided a golden opportunity to empathize with students and envision better ways of teaching and learning and recognizing the best and worst possible way of imparting knowledge. I was excited to see the students who were interested in learning and thinking critically even in a bad teaching and learning setting. Although it was rare, there were at least a handful of students who brought in innovative and critical ways of thinking to tutorial classes and were not afraid to talk about their ideas in front of the others. It was like a gift that I had from a few students in a few classes while many students wanted to know what they were supposed to know so that they could give them back to me as answers during examination time.

This was truly the beginning of the formative years of my teaching career. The lessons that I learnt while working in such a setting where most students were hungry to learn were important. I had the opportunity of developing these ideas further during the time I switched my major discipline of education from history to computer sciences in the U.S. later on in my teaching career.

I had the rare fortune of going through Computer Science graduate school in an entirely different discipline than history and in an entirely different educational set up and system in the U.S. that greatly enhanced my experience in teaching college level courses. Although it was a frustrating experience for me to sit in a classroom listening to lectures once again later in my life after having completed a doctoral degree in history at the University of London U.K., and having taught college courses over 7 years, I had an excellent opportunity to observe various teaching styles practiced by different college professors in teaching their classes; the mistakes made by teachers in college classes provided me with insights on developing my own good habits in college teaching, learning and advisement that greatly helped me throughout my career as a college professor for 25 years in the U.S. Going back to the classroom for three years to earn a graduate degree in computer science after having had a career as a college professor was a blessing in disguise that I had in my college teaching career.

SECTION TWO
Paradigm Shift

College educators constantly attempt to prepare students to be problem solvers and decision makers in all career tracks. In their efforts at addressing these needs, they struggle as to whether they should focus on course content, developing critical thinking, and/or technology skills of students who they train. With the growing emphasis on technology in education during the last three decades, the importance of teaching technological skills to supplement the educational process has drawn the attention of education reformers in a significant way. While most colleges and universities are incorporating technology in their educational mission, teachers are asking if they should conform to the traditional lecture method with a heavy focus on course content and memorization, and developing critical thinking skills among the students or if they should adopt a more outcome-based "learner oriented" approach utilizing technology in education to produce highly skilled workers for the work place.

After hundreds of years of usage, the traditional educational model seems to be under scrutiny by educational reformers and undergoing change. The traditional teacher and the traditional teaching methods are gradually being removed from today's college classrooms. Interestingly, while the role of the traditional teacher seem to be somewhat changing, the role of the student too is undergoing a similar change.

Typically, today's college classrooms have students who take 16-18 credit hours, having a very busy schedule with extra-curricular activities, or in some instances, students devoting over 20 hours a week of work doing service related part-time jobs. Colleges also have non-traditional students, who either come back to college to complete a degree that they did not finish early in life or retrain for new opportunities in the job market. Whatever the case may be, unlike in the past, most students today who are extremely busy tend to have a very short attention span in the classroom and are not necessarily good listeners and not solely bent on learning subject matter in a classroom as they would have been in the past. They have very little patience, and high demand to obtain the required course content that satisfies the degree or certification requirements in the shortest possible time. The ever rising college tuition costs and the heavy debt college students incur as a result of college education are other factors that contribute to the changing role of today's college student.

Amidst the college teacher and the student are the education administrators who are attempting to address the challenges of changing student demography and needs in colleges and universities with increasing operating expenses and decreasing income.

A Paradigm shift:

One of the most used as well as misunderstood terms among educators today, is the term "paradigm shift." the dictionary meaning of paradigm is "a pattern, an example, or a model." A paradigm shift therefore, is a change from one model to another, as it were for example, from an old world-view to a new world-view. The notion of paradigm suggests that people tend to "see" the world in terms of old frameworks and to respond to it within prescribed limits and with familiar skills. During a "paradigm shift" people may be seeing a new world and responding to this new world with tools and practices that are no longer relevant. ref: Thomas Kuhn on paradigm shift https://plato.stanford.edu/entries/thomas-kuhn/

A "paradigm shift" expresses a notion that has a deeper underlying meaning to it that, in a way, could only be understood with a personal realization -- a realization that comes from within a person's inner self, so similar to the attainment of an ecstatic sensation. A "paradigm shift" from the "traditional world" to "a new world", should reflect an inner change that is deeper, so profound, and powerful as well as meaningful to those who are affected by the resultant shift.

It is natural that introducing any kind of change within a system is bound to create challenges and conflicts. Changing existing procedures and practices in institutions that have hundreds of years of tradition, is bound to create enormous problems and conflicts. It is therefore important that the people who work within a system have a good understanding about the goal and the nature of the intended change. There should be an unequivocal agreement on the basic principles of the intended change, and there should be unequivocal commitment among the implementers of change at every level. In short, the change implementers should be prepared to change themselves before they could successfully implement change and shift the system within which they operate. Paradigm shifters are, in a way, similar to self-regulating mechanisms, almost like thermostats that regulate their own function from within and without, in this case, change. In such an environment the only constant is the change itself. Introducing change without its necessary corollary, intrinsic change of the people component who work within the system, is therefore destined to fail.

Implementing Change:

The small class size, ranging from 8 to 25 in all the classes that the author implemented innovative teaching/learning methods created no additional classroom management problems. Further, the flexibility given to "change agents" by the system within which changes were implemented by the author was a motivating factor that encouraged innovative teaching/learning methods without having to worry about violating the established teaching practices. However, the author was cautious not to implement changes so radical and drastic completely different from the existing practices; hence most of the changes were implemented in a graduated fashion.

Following changes were introduced in an unstructured fashion in all the classes taught by the author during the period of 1992 - 1996. Since it was experimentation, a rigid structured method was not chosen.

Implementing Total Quality Education Concepts in the Classroom:

The author practiced his teaching/learning experiments made a commitment to adopting Total Quality Management (TQM) and Total Quality Learning (TQL) at the beginning of the 1990s, in one university system where 11 campuses and colleges were combined as one-university system. Some important changes that followed were:

1. Streamlining university administration under the leadership of a single office – the Chancellor of the University System

2. Commitment to Total Quality Management in University administration by developing a seven year implementation plan.

3. Applying Total Quality concepts in the area of learning by bringing in Total Quality consultants from outside and networking around the country with higher education institutions that apply Total Quality concepts in Higher education.

4. Bringing in volunteers as local campus advisors who had learned the techniques of Total Quality Management and Total Quality teaching and learning methods.

The author's ideas were developed in one of the 11 universities targeted to be eliminated from the system due to economic difficulties and budgetary constraints. Adopting TQM/L was thought of as a working solution to prevent the impending closure.

Introducing a Paradigm Shift in the Classroom:

The following factors helped the author to a large extent in introducing changes in his classroom teaching practices:

a) Changing the existing system was mandated as a top-down decision of the university administration. It was almost similar to a "do or die" situation, b) resistance to change from the sub-systems was minimal, change was encouraged although the enthusiasm for implementing meaningful change was low, especially among the senior faculty members who were almost reaching the age of retirement, c) there were a considerable number of teachers who were motivated and were genuinely interested in implementing innovative ways of doing things, d) some funds were available through educational grants given to facilitate "change agents" to travel and participate in conferences and undergo training that promoted similar interests.

A group of highly enthusiastic faculty members met every week for several hours engaging in discussions and activities that generated innovative ideas for experimenting changes in teaching and learning styles in classrooms and utilizing technology. These collective ideas encouraged the faculty members to introduce changes in the way they teach and promote students to learn without being fearful about changing existing traditions.

To lecture or not to lecture:

Imparting information and knowledge through formal lectures was probably the most popular method of teaching in higher educational institutions form the time of their inception centuries ago. As higher education institutions became more formalized, institutionalized, accessible to the public, and conducted similar to other business enterprises, the use of lecture method to deliver information to large audiences of students also became an important characteristic of our educational system. Consequently, the lecture method continued as the most widely practiced method of teaching in colleges and universities.

In all through the author's career as a college professor for over 40 years, and all his associations with over 10 universities in three different countries in the world, he saw the lecture method of teaching as the primary method of imparting information and knowledge to students. The only exception to this method seen by the author was in one university in Asia, was the tutorial-class system that divided large lecture classes ranging from 100 to 1500 students into smaller classes of about 10 students in each, and moderated by junior faculty members. Such tutorial classes provided an opportunity for each student to actively participate in education by presenting a paper on a given topic related to the lectures for further classroom discussion.

The author in all his under-graduate and graduate schools attended lectures sometimes that lasted for more than two hours at one sitting. He remembers trying to take down notes of everything the professors said. He remembers the days when a blind student in his class struggled to take down notes using a brail machine and also the days when students recorded the lectures using tape recorders and took notes from those tapes.

As university professors, we tend to imitate our professors in our classes. One of my professors in graduate school did not fail to bring a can of soft drink into the classroom and sip it through the lecture in every one of his lecture periods. One professor talked the whole class period and did not stop to find out, even once, if his students understood what he said during the entire lecture or if the students had any questions. But, unfortunately, it was the way the system worked in most teaching environments.

Most students expected their professors to talk the entire class period. The traditional student usually sat in the back of the classroom and listened to the professor's lecture. They made it a habit to ask their professor "what are we going to do today" at the beginning of each class. Obviously, their intention was to quickly find out what the professor wanted them to learn from his lecture of the day for the upcoming quiz or examination, so that they could memorize those things and return them back to the teacher. Breaking this mind-set in a classroom was a challenge that each creative teacher had to face.

Introducing Change in Classroom Management Style:

The traditional classroom management techniques in educational institutions were more or less based on a teacher having absolute control over the students. Such a style is reflected in the Harvard Law Professor's role of the television series "Paper Chase." In the education administrative system, senior teachers not only have a great control on students but also on junior teachers. Therefore, a change in the deep-seated classroom management practices in education was not always easy or pleasant.

As an initial step towards increasing student motivation, the author made a concerted effort to drive away fear from the classroom. The students no longer came to the class because they had to attend the class for their grade.

The author's philosophy of teaching and his expectations from students were made very clear to the students in his handouts given on the very first day of the class in every class he taught. A good part of the first day of class was spent in setting up the "Ground Rules" for the students as well as for the teacher. One activity in the first day of class consisted of finding out the expectations of students and matching them with the expectations of the teacher and curriculum. Student input as to what makes them most happy in college (Appendix I) served the author to understand his class to a great extent.

In addition to using "mini-lectures" the use of textbook, handouts, small group discussions, classroom demonstrations, classroom discussions, field-trips were used as learning resources. The reason for using such a variety of methods and resources was simple: not everyone learned the same way, not at the same rate of speed.

For the most part, the classes were conducted by the author in a seminar fashion with frequent "mini-lectures." The students were expected to come to class fully prepared to participate, both by sharing important data and information and by critically analyzing the contributions of other students in the class in the form of discussions moderated by the teacher.

Since the ultimate goal of education has little to do with rote-learning, memorization was not required in all the courses taught by the author. Books, text-books, notes, and any other material were permitted to be used in all examinations done by the students. The rationale for this decision and practice was that memorization and reproducing memorized material in examinations, lead to no useful advance in learning, problem solving, critical thinking, and application of knowledge except in disciplines where rote memory was extremely important. Moreover, humans tend to forget things committed to memory with the passage of time. In the information age in which we live today, learning how to find the information quickly has become more important than trying to commit all information into human memory, a humanly impossible task. Because of these reasons, the author's focus of learning experience in his classes was not memorization, but developing the skills and ability to find out the needed information and provide the student with the training to critically think and apply the gathered data and information towards problem solving.

As shown in the next section, active participation in the learning process was the primary method of sharing knowledge adopted by the author.

SECTION THREE
Teaming-up for Learning and Doing

Developing teamwork skills is a necessity in today's changing workplace. Work teams are important organizational units in corporations. The demand for employees having communication and teamwork skills in addition to the required technical knowledge and skills has greatly increased as a necessity in the employment sector. If employer demands are to be satisfied by educational institutions, changes ought to be made in the way students are prepared for work life in the academe. Students have to learn new skills within the curricula that we teach, and changes have to be made in the way they are taught, and the performance standards to which they are held.

This chapter discusses the challenges for preparing team workers in the academe, the benefits of incorporating team work in academic curricula, and identifies methods for effectively assessing and evaluating team members' performance as well as outcomes of student team projects involving the application of technology.

The assessing and evaluating methods discussed in this chapter were put into practice in freshman through senior computer information systems classes over a period of six years by the author in two different universities In performing these tasks the author made the following assumptions: a) the expectation of most college students (and their parents too, in some cases) in making an investment in college education is to gain a competitive edge in the employment sector b) most universities, colleges, technical colleges, and community colleges are in competition to cater to this need of prospective students in order to increase enrollment.

Teamwork in industry versus teamwork in the academe:

The environment of the academic world is far different from that of the "work-world." Whereas student performance is not critically important to the ultimate survival of the institution in which the student engage in their learning process, nothing less than their best performance is expected from the employees in the "real-world" work environments. In most academic environments student performance is evaluated by a measuring scheme, in some instances on a curve that compares one student's academic performance with another – a measuring scheme that awards a letter grade A – F. Under such a scheme individual performance is the most important criterion of performance evaluation that tends to produce highly individualistic personalities who believe in attempting to do everything individually and independently.

The tendency in industry however, is to promote employees to work in teams. One most important reason for teamwork is that a team would take less time to perform all the activities and tasks that make up a project than an individual. When projects have to be completed within the shortest period of time in a highly competitive environment, the team that performs the best within the shortest period of time tends to outperform the same work done independently by individuals. In reality this principle applies to both manual and mental work. Therefore, teamwork skills are becoming increasingly important in the competitive corporate world of today.

Team experience in the real world work environment and educational environments (if at all teamwork is practiced in class projects) may mean totally different realities to the team workers. For instance team workers in a production company may feel the stress of losing 1 million dollars a day in interest payment on a loan that finances the project. The survival of an entire company may depend on the success of a project completed on time. A close parallel in the academe could be a research effort of a graduate program in a university. However, graduate research efforts are mostly targeted for publication rather than production efforts. Unlike in the industry, teaming up of students belonging to different disciplines (departments in the case of companies) in team efforts may present difficult challenges in classrooms. Further, teamwork skills cannot be transferred conceptually or in the form of a recipe in a cookbook. Neither can they be acquired individually. How much of teamwork skill-set can be transferred to students in a classroom in an educational environment, is therefore a challenge.

Moreover, the environment in education is very different from the "real-world" work. In both research as well as teaching universities, faculty members are evaluated mostly on their individual performance for the purpose of retention, tenure, promotion in rank etc. as shown in chapters on tenure and promotion discussed in part one of this book. Due to this reason, a very high degree of competition and sometimes, covert rivalry among faculty members may be seen in the academe. Promoting teamwork among students in academic environments could therefore present difficult challenges to most faculty members who may not have had any real world teamwork experience. Besides, teamwork is not regarded as absolutely essential to be successful in an academic environment, especially in research universities.

How teamwork was implemented by the author in class:

Realizing the risks of radically changing an existing system, the author applied teamwork in class in several phases. One of the very first challenges in applying teamwork in classroom was determining how to engage students in teamwork and still preserve the quality of conceptual (content) learning experience that they need to receive from the course material. A course that could easily be adapted for teamwork, senior capstone project course, was selected in 1993 for experimentation. In place of the earlier practice of each student having to complete a project individually in this course, students were required to engage in teamwork, 3-4 students in a team. Introducing "conversations for action" in this class eliminated fifty-minute lectures. The format of the class was as follows: After 10 – 15 minutes of review of material by the instructor, the teams engaged in practical work. All team members were expected to have gained the necessary basic knowledge by getting a C or better grade in the junior level course that leads them to this capstone project course. The requirement for purchasing a textbook for the course was eliminated by using a textbook that sufficiently covered content material for development methods and their applications in the preparatory class that the students had taken during their Junior-year.

Students in the senior capstone course were introduced to group dynamics at the very beginning of the semester. The importance of communication, developing listening and leadership skills, scheduling and time management skills were some of the topics discussed early on before students were engaged in teamwork. Also, having students discuss what they know about themselves, what they do not know about themselves, what others perceive about them that they do not know about, the importance of verbal and non-verbal communications were some of the topics of discussion that promoted success of team projects. Johari Window techniques that improve team workers were introduced to the team workers at the very beginning of team projects (Ref: https://www.google.com/search?sxsrf=ALeKk03uiL8rBVveqjAGa1_T7CcEcINAhA%3A1603983367893&source=hp&ei=B9iaX5jmM5D-4tAW1-an4DQ&q=johari+window&oq=johari&gs_CjoE-CAAQDToHCAAQyQMQDToGCAAQFhAeOgsILhCx-AxDJAxCTAjoFCAAQyQM6BAguEApQ1BBY2NsBY-PjtAWgRcAB4AIABxAGIAZkPkgEENC4xMpgBAKA-BAaoBB2d3cy13aXqwAQo&sclient=psy-ab)

The emphasis of the class was primarily application of the techniques they learned in all other courses and the students were specifically informed of their responsibilities before they engaged in their team project.

The team assumed complete control of the project as outlined by a blueprint they produced during the Junior-year, at the end of their project development methods class. They were made aware that they would be responsible for adhering to the time-line they provided delineating the lifecycle of the project. Each project consisted of a project leader, a scribe (recorder), analyzer, and programmer (as needed depending on the nature of the project). Assessment of the project was done using several criteria. Peer evaluation, periodical written reports regarding the stages of completion, oral presentations at the completion of each activity of the project, observation by the instructor, regular journals kept by individual team members, and the final presentation to a panel of judges that evaluated the team project that considered these criteria. Percentages assigned to each of these criteria were specified to the team at the beginning of the semester. The outcome of the project – a final product with documentation, proved the project team's effort as successful.

What students learn by engaging in teamwork?

As described above, the teamwork experience that students receive in the capstone course and other courses where teamwork was done in partial fulfillment of course requirement provided a very rare and unique experience to students thereby preparing them for the "real-world." Students who completed their teamwork successfully gained the ability to work within a team. This experience may be compared to learning how to ride a bicycle; an experience in "balancing" that cannot be learned by reading a book or from a description of the experience given by a teacher.

Students also learned the importance of time management, scheduling, punctuality, reliability and dependability – important character traits of an engaging team worker. Since each team member's overall contribution to the project was evaluated by the other team members of the project, team members quickly learned to take responsibility of the overall project and they learned that the success of the project depended on each member's contribution. Most importantly, teamwork taught the team members to set a common goal and achieve that goal within a specified period of time. In the process of working in teams, students learned the synergy principle – whole is greater than the sum of its parts. Teamwork enabled team members to complete a project together more efficiently and within a shorter period of time than they could otherwise individually.

Problems encountered:

The successful completion of a project from beginning to end within a single semester presented difficult challenges to both team workers and the instructor. Although the author utilized the junior year preparation class as a basis for the capstone class, there was no assurance that the same group of students would do the capstone course in consecutive semesters. Transfer students and students who had done the preparatory course a few years before, joining in the capstone course presented a difficult situation.

Dealing with "slackers" in teams presented problems to the team members as well as to the instructor. Students who were satisfied with a passing grade of C or D did not have the enthusiasm, time, or desire to fully cooperate with others in teamwork. They were habitually late, uninvolved, and were happy to satisfy the minimum requirements that would give them the lowest possible passing grade.

In some teams there were students who were unable to get along with others, or made it a habit to complain about other team members. There were occasions when some students complained about a team leader who they thought was excessively controlling. Personality conflicts among team members were also frequent occurrences.

In spite of the above-mentioned problems, a considerable number of students benefited from teamwork experience. Team projects enabled the author to realistically assess students' interpersonal communications skills and their ability to function as team members. Most importantly, team work gave students a rare opportunity to prepare themselves for real world work.

Ideas for improving teamwork techniques:

Implementing teamwork in classes is not a smooth transition from the traditional lecture method of teaching to teaming up students to learn on their own. Every class in every discipline may not be suitable for student teamwork. Depending on the discipline in which teamwork is implemented, and depending on the overall goal of providing teamwork experience to students, instructors may need to have experience in having done teamwork, and experience in dealing with conflict resolution preferably in the industry. Most importantly, educational institutions implementing innovation in teaching, such as using teamwork as a vehicle for practical experience for students, need to have an understanding and appreciation of teamwork and how teamwork would benefit students in their future employment, before they apply teamwork in classes. Disagreement among faculty regarding the overall benefits of such innovations may only create dissention among the faculty.

The elements of teamwork skills that team members share in industrial settings, especially the experience shared by high performance teams, cannot be conceptually transferred easily in an academic environment. The closest parallel could be collaborative projects between university faculty and companies in which student teams may be engaged. Assessment schemes that eliminate or substitute examinations by criteria that enhance synergy among team members may therefore pose challenges to both instructors and students in an academic environment. Addressing these challenges successfully would necessitate a paradigm shift in the way the instructors teach and in the way students learn.

Overall, this style of learning highlights an assessment and evaluation method based on outcomes of teamwork discussed in the next section which is a measurement scheme that is significantly different from the traditional "course-credit-completion" method that measures students' performance on a curve.

SECTION FOUR
Outcome-based Teaching and Learning

Learning outcomes specify the observable and /or measurable knowledge, skills and ability to make decisions based on data, which a student is expected to have developed or acquired as the result of a course of study designed on a set of identifiable goals or experiences. They are about what a person should know or be able to do or demonstrate after completing a program of study.

Identifying learning outcomes is a challenge that requires planning and detailing what a teacher expects a student to achieve, and the level of that achievement rather than simply describing what a teacher intends to teach or cover in a syllabus. Clearly defining course outcomes is a continuous process of improvement of learning.

The enthusiasm for course outcomes among educators reflects a significant shift of emphasis from a syllabus-driven educational inputs, content, and time allocation, to results. The shift is off teaching to learning that emphasizes outcomes of learning rather the process of learning itself. Consequently, defining and identifying course outcomes for college/university courses have became an important educational tool to assess and validate the leaning experience and performance levels of the learners.

The Challenge:

Today, both students and employers demand specific technical skills to be provided by higher educational institutions to their consumers. Both the consumers and providers of higher education are living in an increasingly competitive environment in which the access of outcome-based learning is making the higher education market attractive to employers. Consequently, learning outcomes, as measured by student competencies, have become a quality measure that makes the most sense to students, educators as well as employers.

Educators try to validate the effectiveness of the learning experience of their students by asking such questions as "how do we know that the students comprehend the material delivered in the classroom?", "what do we want students to be able to do from their learning experience that they gain from the course after they graduate and join the workforce?" Technology-based disciplines mostly impacted by the rapid changes in technology present greater challenges as well as positive responses to educators when it comes to providing a quality education to learners.

Benjamin Bloom identified six levels within the cognitive domain (of human learning experience), each becoming increasingly complex and abstract. These are knowledge, comprehension, application, analysis, synthesis, and evaluation. (Ref: https://www.bloomstaxonomy.net/Blooms Taxonomy :: Resource for Educators)). Proper planning and determination of the expected outcomes that are closely associated with each of these levels would enable developing assessment rubrics that would help teachers to assess and evaluate the quality of learning and communicate expected levels of learning to their students. Outcome-based teaching and learning methods that are closely linked with assessment techniques based on learning outcome levels therefore provides the evaluators a better understanding of students' learning experience. The author considers most technology-based disciplines that are impacted by the constant growth and development of technology and information are ideal grounds for outcome-based teaching and learning.

A logical starting point of writing outcomes for any course would be an examination of the program/department/college/university mission. Obviously, the beliefs of the writers of outcomes will have an impact on the course outcomes they identify and define in detail. Nevertheless, they need to ask questions like, "What do we want students to learn throughout this course?" and "What do we want students in our courses to continue to know five or ten years after completing the course?" Such questions would enable them to determine what the graduates of the program should know, what skills they should be able to demonstrate and what professional values they should hold. A general list of expected objectives for graduates could be generated from such an exercise. Converting this list into statements of specific learning outcomes and how these outcomes are achieved consist of the next step while the actual writing of the course outcomes is the very last step of this process.

As an example, a possible general list of the course objectives for a semester-based course curriculum for an undergraduate course in systems analysis and design course could be, but not limited to the following topics:

- Describe the role of the systems analyst.
- Demonstrate the skills used in structured design methodologies using CASE (Computer Aided Software Engineering) tools.
- Use proper techniques in completing a feasibility study.
- Describe the techniques used to conduct investigative systems interviews.
- Define and use valid documentation techniques.
- Design internal and external auditing controls.
- Design system and information flows.
- Design system inputs such as forms and display screens.
- Design system outputs such as specialty forms, reports, and print-screens.
- Design system data sets and define relationships among records and files.
- Write appropriate narratives as required – management, system and user documents
- Design and implement a prototype of the designed system using CASE or other prototyping tools.
- Design several implementation plans for the system and select the most suitable one (with justification) for the environment in which the system would be implemented.

Once a list of objectives has been identified, the next step would be to convert them into statements of specific learning outcomes by describing how these outcomes are to be achieved.

Linking Course Outcomes to Assessment:

If student outcomes are about the actual learning, students should exhibit such an outcome as a result of planned learning experiences. The accountability mechanisms that directly reflect student performance are the validating tools of outcome-based education. Accordingly, educational structures and curricula should be regarded as means and not ends of learning, and if they do not do the job they are intended for, they need to be rethought and re-worked.

One key feature of assessment of student learning through outcomes method is that the students are made clear about the expectations for learning outcomes, and the expectations of them to work outside of the classroom in order to meet the outcomes. The acceptable level of achievement of learning outcomes forms an integral part of this method. For example, a low-level target achievement might be the ability of the student to accurately repeat what has been given, while a high-level target might be the ability of the student to go beyond the knowledge of the information given. However, it is vital that the students are well aware of the expectations for achievement in order to obtain the best results by demonstrating their ability to perform the tasks/functions at the level/standard determined and outlined at the very beginning of the learning experience.

Quantitative and Qualitative Assessments:

While quantitative assessment enables educators to gather numerical data relating to student learning, qualitative assessments provide other observable, indirect and descriptive evidence of student learning. Selecting an appropriate assessment method depends on the learning outcomes identified in the program.

The author uses multiple assessment methods listed below to validate students' ability to perform the learning outcomes identified in the selected course as given below.

Quantitative	Qualitative
Pre-test/Post-test evaluation	Teamwork
Un-announced quizzes	Timely submission of projects
Submission of homework on due dates	Presentations (both individual and in groups).
Mid-term exams	Field experiences
	Weekly journals
	Project planning and management
	Leadership and participation
	Outside reading and research
	Student surveys and interviews
	Exit interviews
	Observations made by the instructor
	Peer evaluations

Unlike quantitative methods of assessment, qualitative assessment methods are time consuming and require consistent efforts on the part of both teachers and learners. Performance outcomes can be assessed across various attributes of performance using a rubric for each attribute at various levels. These performance tasks can be students' ability to understand a complex problem by analysis, find solution/s to a given problem, giving an effective oral presentation, practice performance in a professional role such as of a systems analyst, ability to produce results on time under stressful circumstances etc. The specific attributes applied to a set of rubrics can be scored individually and summed together or an overall performance score may be generated.

Qualitative assessment measures are not limited to a few exams; active participation of the learners in the learning process and their ability to exhibit competence in more than one way tends to constantly validate not only the learning experience but the ability to apply the knowledge gained as a result of the learning experience.

As an example, students ability to perform the functions of a selected list activities after completing a Systems Design course. Students that actively participate in these activities go through the following steps systematically: 1) understand the requirement 2) gather data 3) analyze the data 4) evaluate the data 5) formulate the solution and 6) communicate the solution to others in an efficient and effective manner. The author uses these activities for not only to assess but to validate students' ability to produce learning outcomes at higher levels of Blooms Taxonomy.

Course outcomes enable us to expand in specific detail a general list of course objectives. They also enable us to identify the ways in which such outcomes are achieved. The resulting list of outcomes that are closely associated with each course objective serves as a common "roadmap" for facilitators of learning as well as those who are engaged in the learning process. Linked with the quantitative and qualitative assessment criteria, these detailed outcomes provide a measuring mechanism that not only lends itself for validation but also for continuous improvement of learning.

A sample course outcome adopted by the author will be given in Appendix II

SECTION FIVE
Critical Thinking
Teaching how to think

In an educational environment in which the traditional classroom is in transition, instructors need to find creative methods to challenge students to engage in certain expected learning experiences to satisfy the guidelines set by curricula. This task involves teaching to think analytically which is a challenging endeavor.

The author adopted the following different methods in an attempt to promote analytical thinking by actively engaging the students in a learning experience different from traditional pedagogy. These methods were: 1) adopting a non-traditional learner-centered style instead of a teacher controlled lecture-based pedagogical style 2) using documentation and journal-writing to enhance analytical thinking 3) using class projects and team work to enhance analytical thinking 4) using a pro-technology assessment/evaluation and grading techniques including peer evaluations that promote student learning, and 5) using online classroom management tool/s to deliver content material for further discussions and other daily announcements.

A discussion of each of these methods follows in the rest of this chapter.

Adopting a Non-Traditional "Learner-Oriented" Teaching Style to Promote Thinking:

In author's opinion, continuing to use traditional teaching methods in a technology-savvy and pro-technology environment would eventually prove to be an ineffective and unproductive exercise. Therefore, the author emphasized learning rather than teaching, assessment rather than evaluation, continuous process improvement (CPI), and lifelong learning as measurements for promoting leaning with technology.

Content delivery using lectures was minimized. Examinations were focused on analytical thinking and not on rote memorization. Students were encouraged to use textbooks during examinations. The main emphasis in a given class was to make connections with the content material relevant to the topic of the day as stipulated in the course schedule. Students were expected to read and understand the recommended content material before attending class. The main topic of discussion on a given day was posted on the Blackboard Course Info, allowing students the opportunity to read, understand, and analyze the material before class. This method of teaching encouraged independence and accountability, while improving the depth of discussion on any given topic. Furthermore, this method of electronic content delivery, if carefully read and understood by the students, saved a considerable amount of class time compared to the more traditional lecture method of teaching.

Using Documentation and Journal-Writing to Enhance Analytical Thinking:

Writing is a great stimulator of thinking. As we struggle with writing we also struggles with thinking. The implementation of a mandatory writing requirement in the course served several purposes, including the development of innovative ideas and concepts, organization and documentation of those ideas, communication, and a method of analyzing one's own thought. Writing was encouraged through the use of assigned 'micro-themes,' a minute paper demanding a very short definition of a concept, at the beginning or end of a class. This assignment probed student minds, enhanced class participation, and promoted thinking, while determining students' cognitive skill levels regarding a selected topic. Subsequent to the writing phase, a classroom discussion phase occurred in class, where students were asked to critically analyze their peers' work in an open discussion format. While the practice of writing micro-themes gave every student in class an opportunity to participate in a collective process, the immediate feedback given to randomly selected 'micro-themes' written by students served as an effective way to engage students' attention and active participation in a classroom discussion.

Another method of challenging students to think and actively participate in the learning process was by engaging them to brain storming sessions and commit to writing answers to questions relating to the assigned text material scheduled for the day. This method encouraged students to be accountable for their own education and read the textbook before attending class. The author utilized writing to encourage students to prepare ahead by doing the required reading, to participate in brainstorming sessions in class, and finally to submit their work in written form to the critical review of their peers.

It was the author's observation that the habit of regular writing in class helped students to make connections with the textbook chapter material relating to the day's schedule. Students were encouraged to keep journals of their daily class activities in a separate folder that they maintained on their laptops. Such journals enabled them to take control of their own learning. The author's daily journals relating to the class were placed in Blackboard Course Info daily announcements that reached students before each class on a regular basis. These journals were accessible to students at all times through their laptops.

Using Class Projects and Teamwork to Enhance Analytical Thinking:

Can analytical thinking be taught? Is thinking teachable? Can thinking be promoted online in an asynchronous format? Does every student think in the same way? Does the type of formal training received make someone think in a particular way? Can higher order thinking be taught with technology? These and many other questions relating to thinking made the "teaching" of analytical thinking a complex task.

Facing all of these questions became a reality in the classes that students participated in teamwork either in person or online. Unless the students were willing to think, thinking did not occur. This is true in any problem-solving environment in which the problem solver will have to be willing to study the problem at hand, understand it by gathering all available information and formulate a problem-solving plan. This process involves intensive thinking, which is dependent upon the complexity of the problem intended to be solved. The experience in having thought through similar problems gives an added advantage to the problem solver in recognizing patterns that eventually helped to solve a problem quickly and efficiently. For example, an experienced systems analyst may therefore be able to guide a novice in systematic thinking patterns more effectively than a person who has had no experience as a systems analyst in the real world. Brainstorming and discussing problems in teams may therefore promote experienced systems analysts to transfer their knowledge and experience to novices.

Realizing the difficulty of radically changing an existing system, the author incorporated the teamwork approach to his classes in several phases. One of the very first challenges in applying teamwork in the classroom was determining how to engage students in teamwork while still preserving the quality of conceptual learning experience that they must receive from the course. With active communication among team members in mind, the author changed the seating arrangement of the classroom so that students would face each other, instead of facing the teacher or the computer, to facilitate active discussions, brainstorming, and practice group thinking sessions. The groups were allowed to select leaders, recorders and presenters. They were also encouraged to use technology to communicate by email, record their thinking patterns with word processors, create graphics using technology, and schedule and create project documentation using MS Project.

Using a Pro-Technology Assessment/Evaluation and Grading Techniques including Peer Evaluations that Promoted Student Learning:

Many scholars have done research on assessment, evaluation, grading, and other methods of measuring student learning. While there is considerable debate as to which method of evaluation maximizes students' learning experiences, the author's classroom assessment and evaluation practices were based on the hypothesis that the essence of the learning experience should remain the same no matter which method is used to reach its goal (i.e. higher order analytical thinking).

Distributing the grade points over a variety of activities that students were required to engage in on a regular basis was one method the author used to encourage active participation of students in the learning process. A point scheme giving a certain percentage of the total grade for teamwork was one way in which students' active participation was ensured. Assessment and evaluation of the projects were done using several criteria: 1) peer evaluation 2) periodical written reports 3) class discussions 4) observation by the instructor 5) regular journals kept by individual team members, and 6) presentation of project outcomes to a panel of judges. Percentages assigned to each of these criteria were specified to teams at the beginning of each team activity. Each team was required to evaluate and grade other teams' work. Evaluating teams had to first come up with evaluation criteria before they began the evaluation process. The evaluation criteria were required to be consistent with the standard criteria given in the literature.

In addition to these methods, the author gave a list of the likely questions they would be asked during the final examination as an incentive to study and learn the material in the textbook. Students were required to find answers to the questions individually, brainstorm their answers in their respective groups, and make modifications as needed. At the end of a brain storming session, the author facilitated a group discussion where randomly selected answers were presented by members of different teams to the entire class. This was an opportunity for each student in the class to participate and discuss answers regarding: a) the depth of understanding of the problem b) the gathering, organization, and analysis of relevant data, and c) the solution presented. These discussion groups indirectly helped students to evaluate their own answers. Although the available time for such classroom activities was limited, this process enabled the entire class to concentrate on a single problem and formulate a comprehensive solution. However, the success of this process in promoting analytical thinking mainly depended on the preparation, participation and motivation level of the class as a whole entity, and more importantly, the maturity level of students.

Using online classroom management tool/s to deliver content material for further discussions and other daily announcements:

The author started using online teaching platforms including Top-Class (1997), Web-CT (1998), and Blackboard Course Info (1999-2001). His experience gained from online teaching was that not every student engages in the learning process in the same way.

Beginning in year 2001, the author adopted Blackboard Course Info for online classroom management. He used this facility to deliver course content material and all daily announcements relating to the class online. Some advantages of using this classroom management package were: a) the ability to communicate with students regularly on a daily basis regarding learning activities related to a class b) the ability to send topics and summaries of content material that students were expected to review before they arrive in class c) the ability to perform assessments using true/false questions and essay type answers that would give instant feedback d) the ability to reach students who are unable to make it to class and e) the ability to archive all classroom material in one place a synchronically that is accessible to students 24 hours a day 7 days a week.

In online teaching, Hybrid or partially and online classroom were clearly defined.

It must be mentioned in this respect that one critical success factor of any online teaching/learning environment is the learner' motivation to learn. Unfortunately, most students are motivated by their desire to obtain a good grade, and learning activities which are not tightly coupled with a grading scheme that assigns points for their successful completion of tasks by the students are not perceived by them as valuable. These students would be less likely to attend a rigorous classroom discussion if they were not awarded points for attending or participating in class discussions. Unless attendance in the class was made mandatory and an integral part of their grade, students usually did not attend classes regularly. The author conducted online classes having taken these challenges into consideration.

SECTION SIX
Epilogue
Some Reflections on Best Practices of Teaching and Learning

Grading

Grading system is the commonly accepted method of classifying students' learning capability by categorizing them into A, B, C, D or F grade students. While there has been discussions over the pros and cons of the grading system in education among educators, education administrators and employers, grading system is still the largely accepted method of evaluating, assessing or judging student learning capabilities, knowledge, performance level and above all, employability.

One of the most important criteria in admission to colleges today is the grade point average of an applicant. Similarly, most employers carefully look at the grade point average of their applicants during their hiring process.

Consequently, grades have not only become an integral part of the educational system, but also more important than education per se. Consequently, receiving a grade in the classroom has become the primary reason for most students for attending classes in colleges and universities.

As shown in the chapter on classroom management, a teacher has the complete control over the students in a classroom as well as the grade they are given at the end of a semester's course-work. The senior the teacher is in his/her rank, the more control the teacher has over the student/s; depending on their seniority and reputation in an institution, they also have the advantage of having the administrators on their side. No amount of complaints regarding bad teaching, injustice, and/or unfair treatment, even in case where students are bold enough to run the risk of making a complaint to administration, can make any significant impact regarding such a teacher's attitude towards or grades given by them to students.

Unfortunately, course grades are not appropriate indicators of learning outcomes. A course grade only reflects a letter (A,B,C,D,F) assigned by the instructor to a student for a course taken at the end of a semester. In the planning and preparation for teaching a course, the instructor decides on certain defined activities that will be graded. These defined activities may include quizzes, homework, mid-term or final examinations, projects etc. Each of these defined activities is a limited sample of student learning, knowledge, and performance capability. These limited samples of student learning are then summarized into a single letter grade. The letter is a composite or a representative summary of activities of the student during a given semester. Therefore, some educators tend to think that student portfolios serve a better purpose for assessing student learning in a more comprehensive way. In educational programs where submission of portfolios are required for awarding a passing grade for a course, students are expected to integrate, extend, critique and apply the knowledge they acquired in their major course of study.

Other important considerations:

When the intended goal of the learning experience is not to reproduce textbook material through memorization, fewer students make it a habit to read textbook material in preparation for a class except for an examination. Likewise, when exams are open book, most students read the textbook at the last minute or while taking the examination. However well intended, open book exams invariably result in defeating the very purpose of learning – most students copy answers right out of the textbook, some e-mail their answers to other students. The tendency among most online instructors today is not to pay much attention to online cheating, thereby trusting that the online students engage in doing an honest and responsible job of learning.

A classroom environment in which each student has a laptop computer in front of her/him has provided the students with a device to shield them from the rest of the students in the classroom. The author has often noticed students in his class engaged in performing work related to other classes online, sending and receiving e-mail, navigating favorite web sites, maintaining their own web site, and doing business on eBay.

Attempting to harness the capabilities of digital interfaces a mistake is often made by online educators by trying to recreate the same classroom-teaching model in an online environment. Unfortunately, an online teaching method designed to mimic the traditional classroom teaching style becomes a restriction and a barrier to the teacher's ability to impart knowledge.

Finding the "middle ground" amidst this changing face of the "face-to-face classroom" to "a fully/partially/web-enhanced/web-enabled/hybrid online classroom" and at the same time rendering a justice to education could perhaps present enormous challenges to educators of today and tomorrow.

REFERENCES:

1. T. Angelo and K.P Cross, Classroom Assessment Techniques: A Handbook for College Teachers (1993)

2. Thomas A. Angelo and K. Patricia Cross, Classroom Assessment Techniques, Jossey-Bass Publishers, 1993.

3. Janice H. Patterson and Marshall S. Smith, *The Role of Computers in Higher Order Thinking, a paper prepared for inclusion in the 1985 Yearbook for the National Society for the Study of Education,* Wisconsin Center for Education Research, *p.17*

4. Syllabus, New Dimensions in Education, *Changing the Interface of Education,*

NOVEMBER 2001, VOL. 15, NO. 4

5. Grolund, N.E. (2000). How to write and Use Instructional Objectives (6th ed.). Upper Saddle River, NJ: Prentice-Hall Inc.
6. The 7 Habits of Highly Effective People, Stephen R. Covey, Simpson & Schuster, 1990.

7. The Quality School Managing Students Without Coercion, William Glasser, M.D., Harper Perennial, 1992

APPENDIX 1

Given below are responses given by students in two different classes of two different colleges to the question "what makes me happy" at the end of completing the very first day of class.

Responses given in a morning class

1. spending time with my family

2. my family

3. no homework

4. the feeling of being the best I can be at a certain thing

5. having enough time to exercise 4 times a week

6. accomplishments and conquering a goal

7. getting A's in all my classes

8. weekends

9. Jesus died for me

10. getting my work done early so I can relax

11. driving Porsches

12. no homework

13. having a lot of money

14. just to be in class to learn how to do COBOL

15. experiencing new things

16. not losing things my boys and husband, actually picking up after themselves

17. being in the comfort of friends.

18. You are only unhappy when your goal is impossible or you want to be unhappy.

19. Tests are unhappy when it is impossible to get an "A".

20. Mothers-in-laws make people unhappy because they are impossible to get along with.

21. Being around fun people, playing sports, being with my family, doing things for other people, learning information that will help me in life. I am easily amused.

22. Whatever suits me best in a situation makes me happy. I usually "go with the flow", therefore I am usually not disappointed.

23. To be content with my life.

24. Spending time with my children, spending time with my boyfriend of 6 years & last but NOT least learning things & making good grades here in college, and maybe having a few minutes to myself at the end of each day.

25. Being able to come to class and learn the materials.

26. I also have a wonderful husband and son who make me happy as well as my belief in God and going to church every weekend.

27. I love to surf the Web and learn new things about the Web. As a rule I am generally a happy person.

28. My husband and children make me happy.

29. I am happy when I achieve the goals I set for myself, such as getting good grades, passing classes, and eventually finding the RN programs.

30. I am happy to know that by attending school I am making life better for my family.

Responses given in an afternoon class

1. The biggest thing in my life that makes me happy is my children & my husband.

My family is very important to me.

2. Their health and happiness is what makes me happy.

3. By the way, I would also be very pleased to make good grades in all my classes so I don't have to retake any of them.

4. Summer makes me happy.

5. What makes me happy is my daughter, Deserea. She is the most wonderful thing in my life, and is at the very center of everything I do. Going to school, working in the library, every goal that I have, makes me happy. All these goals are for my daughter and her future.

6. My daughter and success ultimately are what makes me happy.

7. I am a Christian, so being "right with the Lord" brings extreme joy to my life.

8. I am engaged to be married and being around a talking to my fiancée makes me happy.

9. I have a good relationship with my parents. Making them proud of me makes me happy. Of course doing well in school and accomplishing something new or difficult makes me happy.

10. I have learned that it doesn't take much to make me happy.

11. I guess the most important necessity to my happiness is love from family and friends. Also, nothing is better than proving to myself that I can do most anything I want, if I work hard enough and want it to happen.

12. My daughter makes me happy. Everything I do – I do it for her and that is why I anticipate on doing good because I am not sure doing it for myself but for her. I guess seeing her makes me happy.

13. I wish I could answer this, I don't really know. I enjoy being with & playing with my daughter, I enjoy engaging in a good conversation about life.

14. I enjoy & appreciate Mother Nature (her power and beauty and strength to adapt). I enjoy crafts, to make things.

15. What makes me happy is God, my family.

16. I am happy when I feel that I am able to learn and express intelligence in personal relationships and helping my fellow man.

17. Feeling like I have learned something after a class is over. At times, a teacher that makes me feels comfortable helps.

18. No stress makes me happy.

19. Learning, teaching, working, gardening, loving, a strong family, church, living in such a wonderful area

20. Watching basketball games; taking classes that I enjoy; hunting & fishing, being with my family; being on the computer

21. My little girl

22. Making good grades, learning, spending time with my future wife, etc.

23. My daughter makes me happy, so does my husband, and not having to worry

24. Learning new things

25. Having a feeling that I have done good at something. I also like to make other people happy

26. Life makes me happy. My family makes me happy

27. I am happy playing with my cousin's 4 children or helping out at a local Nursing Home where my grandmother lives. I am happy with a good book.

28. Learning new things

29. Jesus, family, living life and learning

30. Family, Friends, Money

31. It doesn't take much to make me happy. If everybody is having a good time I will too. I am pretty easy going.

32. Succeed at things

33. Gained knowledge

APPENDIX II
Course CIS 330

Text and Materials:

A suitable text book recommended by the author that covers Computer systems analysis and design.

Description:

The first course in structured methods of identifying the requirements for a system. This includes the analysis of current business operations and definitions of specific problems or opportunities. Goals, objectives, data, process design, and performance criteria are developed for the new systems. Fulfils General Education "writing intensive course" requirements.

Course outcomes:

Upon successful completion of this course, the student will:

- Describe the role of the systems analyst.

- Demonstrate the skills used in structured design methodologies using CASE (Computer Aided System Engineering) tools.
- Use proper techniques in completing a feasibility study.
- Describe the techniques used and conduct investigative systems interviews.
- Define and use valid documentation techniques.
- Design internal and external auditing controls.
- Design system and information flows.
- Design system inputs such as forms and display screens.
- Design system outputs such as specialty forms, reports, and print screens.
- Design system data sets and define relationships among records and files.
- Write appropriate narratives as required – management, system and user documents
- Design and implement a prototype of the designed system using CASE or other prototyping tools.
- Design several implementation plans for the system and select the most suitable one (with justification) for the environment in which the system would be implemented.

Course Objectives	How Addressed	Outcomes	How Measured
1. Describe the role of the systems analyst	Lectures, based on Introduction to Systems Analysis and Design" recommended text material examples and discussion, Web search for information on systems analysts tasks and roles in various companies.	a) Student's ability to describe the job description, functions, and the role played by Systems Analysts in different business environments b) Student's ability to write a job description for a specific company c) student's ability to play the role (role play) of a systems analyst as required by the instructor	Questions that measure a) knowledge b) understanding c) application d) analytical cognition levels

| 2. Demonstrate the skills used in structured design methodologies using CASE tools | Lectures, examples and demonstrations of CASE tools like MS VISIO, and discussion of the relevance of using such tools for communicating complex concepts, based on recommended text book material | Students ability to: a) describe the importance of CASE tools in systems design b) learn and use a selected CASE tool c) analyze a given system design d) draw a simple design for a verbal description of a system provided by the instructor | Ability to: a) represent complex systems using standard diagramming symbols b) correctness of diagrams produced by the student c) provide a verbal description (walk-through) of a system diagram randomly selected by the instructor |

| 3. Define and use valid documentation techniques | Lectures, examples class discussion, and case study assignment, based on the recommended text book material | Students ability to: a) describe the importance of CASE tools in systems design b) learn and use a selected CASE tool c) analyze a given system design d) draw a simple design for a verbal description of a system provided by the instructor | a) Assessment of homework assignments on different types of documentations used and generated by systems analysts b) assessment of the correctness of answers on questions relating to documentation |

4. Use proper techniques in completing a feasibility study	Lectures, examples and class discussion. Case study on feasibility – based on the recommended text book material	Students ability to: a) comprehend the necessity and what is involved in completing a feasibility study b) analyze a given feasibility study c) do a feasibility study and produce the results within a specified period of time.	Evaluation of the feasibility group project for a) data gathering b) depth of requirements analysis c) technical writing capability and following given guidelines d) timeliness of delivery of the feasibility report
5. Understand Systems requirements	Lectures based on recommended text book material	Student's ability to use fact finding techniques such as interviews, questionnaires, surveys, observations etc.	Student's ability to perform the tasks of fact finding in real-life situations

6. Model system and information flows using traditional methods	Lectures, examples class discussion, and case study on DFDs and E-R diagrams, based on recommended text book material	Student's ability to: a) draw data flow diagrams and Entity Relationship diagrams for a given system b) narrate the data and process flows of a DFD or E-R diagram randomly selected by the instructor	Assessment of: a) homework assignments, b) answers to exam questions c) accuracy of DFD's and E-R diagrams produced by students as answer to given assignments
7. Model system and information flows using object oriented methods	Lectures, example, and class discussion based on recommended text book material	Student's ability to: a) represent systems using object oriented techniques	Assessment of homework, case study, and ability to accurately represent a given system using object oriented modeling techniques

8. Design system inputs such as forms and input screens and output reports	Lectures, examples, and class discussion relating to "User Interface, Input, and Output Design"	Students' ability to: a) shift from analysis to design phase b) design input screens and output formats	Students' ability to apply best practices of input and output design by actually engaging in producing input and output screens. Assessment of such student work for correctness and user friendliness
9. Plan application architecture	Lectures, examples, class discussion based on recommended text book material for the course	Students' ability to: a) do the case studies at the end of the chapter b) plan application architecture for any given business environment	Assessment of student case studies for correctness. Assessment of students' knowledge by quizzes and exams

CPSIA information can be obtained
at www.ICGtesting.com
Printed in the USA
LVHW030842030223
738377LV00001B/111

9 781647 493837